CONTEMPORARY DISCOURSES IN NEW LITERATURE

DR. MUZAFFAR A. BHATT | DR. GHANSHYAM PAL & DR.KUMAR GAURAV

To the readers ....

Contents

Acknowledgements

We thank God for being so merciful and gracious. Nothing in the world can be accomplished single handedly, so was true in the process of formulating this important book. We owe deep respect and thanks to many. We undertake this marvelous opportunity to acknowledge our deepest sense of gratitude to our mentors for their consistent encouragement, Positive criticism, interest and guidance have undoubtedly helped us throughout the journey of writing this book. It is proud and eternal privilege for us to record our cordial and sincere gratitude and indebtness to our faculty members of English department Lovely Professional University for their moral support and whole hearted cooperation. We feel honored to extend our gratitude for the valuable suggestions rendered by Dean of School Prof. Pavitar Prakash Singh and our Head of the department Prof. Ajoy Bhatta.

Acknowledgements

[illegible]

Preface

This volume on postmodern and postcolonial crosscurrents in the contemporary literature is an attempt to bring to the fore one of the most controversial issues in the literary, theoretical, and social scenes. The controversy is not so much due to a shortage of definitions about the two movements, but rather to the fact that they are rarely defined precisely enough, leaving room for diverse interpretations to ensue. No consensus, is found among theorists about what postmodernism really means, what its origins are, and whether there are specific traits that allow one to designate postmodernism as really postmodern. Attention is more particularly drawn to the various paradigms attributed to the postmodern phenomenon as a framework for newly emerging modes of intellectual and artistic expression.

In *The Postmodern Turn* (1987), Ihab Hassan presents more than 65 names that literary theorists, psychoanalysts, and social scientists, of various disciplinary backgrounds have provided, covering a range of assumptions about postmodernism, and concludes that such names are 'far too heterogeneous to form a movement [...] or school'. However, this plurality and multiplicity that surrounds the postmodern, and latterly the postcolonial, does not mean that the two cannot be assimilated or come together under one theoretical umbrella. The labels postmodernism and postcolonialism have markedly been employed to refer to two distinct, yet similar, literary and cultural movements that have broken with a now historic instrumentalized modernism and oppressive colonialism. In other words, the two movements apply several theories of innovation, renovation, or change that allow them to go beyond the static conservatism characteristic of imperialist culture and its totalizing systems of representation.

In her important book, *Other Worlds: Essays in Cultural Politics,* Gayatri Spivak notes: "There is an affinity between the imperialist subject and the subject of humanism" (202). While postcolonial thought, motivated by its emerging theory of agency and the existential thrust of identity formation, takes the first as its object of critique, postmodernism largely finds in the second a vast space for scrutinizing the totalizing manifestations of European, and more generally, Western post-industrial culture. This is perhaps to suggest that the prefix "post" in both the postmodern and the postcolonial implies a challenge to the past and an invocation of the notion of history. History, as Ihab Hassan observes in his essay "Toward a Concept of Postmodernism", moves in a direction, "continuous and discontinuous", which means that the prevalence, if any, of postmodernity and/or postcoloniality does not mean that the past ceases to influence or to be influenced by the present moment altogether. The past functions for both postmodern and postcolonial theory and criticism as documentary material fraught with multiple forms of deficiency, oppression, repression, excess, misrepresentation, and misconception. Hence, the replaying of history out of context, as a process, highlights the real crisis of representation that lies at the centre of both the postmodern and the postcolonial. What is in crisis, in fact, is the dominant paradigm of literary and cultural studies and their corollary systems of representation. The text, being a cluster of signs and symbols, therefore, becomes an arena for the expression and debunking of opinion.

The impetus in literary studies to challenge the past came from different directions, primarily from those hermeneutical procedures spearheaded by the new methodologies of cultural poetics/new historicism, deconstruction, feminism, cultural materialism, revisionist criticism, and, most importantly, postmodernism and postcolonialism. In fact, what brings the two movements together is the discourse of oppositionality they bring into being by operating both recursively and subversively. They operate recursively by recurring to the past and engaging with canonical and representative texts and subversively by unravelling such texts and turning them upside down and inside out like a wet sock. Here, I capitalize on the motif of "re-writing" as a key feature and an essential component of both postmodern and postcolonial discourses. Based on the post-Marxist theorist Frederic Jameson's conception of the postmodern/postcolonial era as marked by reproduction rather than production and recreation rather than creation, as well as on Jean-François Lyotard's claim in *The Postmodern Condition: A Report on Knowledge* that the great hero of previous epochs (and I think here he means among others Shakespeare) is no longer a credible figure in the postmodern period, the phenomenon of re-writing, therefore, emerges as a recent practice that is textually and contextually bound to the postmodern/postcolonial condition.

In fact, many factors could be used to demonstrate the confluences between the postmodern and postcolonial enterprises regarding the nature of their discourses and their relationship to the concept of history. First, the major project of postmodernism, which, according to Bill Ashcroft, Gareth Griffiths and Tiffin Helen in *The Empire Writes Back* to the Center, is "the deconstruction of the centralized, logocentric master-narratives of Western culture" (12) overlaps with that of postcolonialism, which is "to dismantle the center-margin binarism of the imperialist discourse". Second, the general crisis over representation resulting from the collapse of the former European empires and from incredulity toward the masternarrative apparatus of legitimation has led to a pressing demand for the reworking of existing literary and cultural material and the disruption of its cognitive bases. Arif Dirlic, who studies the relationship between the postmodern and the postcolonial in terms of the maternal link between the two, contends that "postcolonialism is a child of postmodernism" (8). As such, I borrow from him the "maternal" label to signal the link between the practice of subversive rewriting and the postmodern/postcolonial condition. In a more precise vein, revisionism is a form of subversive rewriting, as a child born of the circumstances characterizing this condition. Two factors intersect that can account for the relationship between the practice of reorienting the past (here referring to Shakespeare as an example) and the postmodern/postcolonial condition. First, postmodern theorists, according to Hannah Berry, realize, as do postcolonialists, that the past must be revised and refashioned into the structure of the present. Second, the major project of postmodernism, which, according to Bill Ashcroft, Gareth Griffiths and Tiffin Helen in *The Empire Writes Back* to the Center, is "the deconstruction of the centralized, logocentric master-narratives of Western culture" (12) overlaps that of postcolonialism, which is "to dismantle the center-margin binarism of the imperialist discourse" (23). By both deconstructing and dismantling, the two movements take on the mantle of destabilizing and re-orienting a certain point of authority. The post-Marxist theorist Frederic Jameson describes the postmodern/postcolonial condition as a phase of reproduction rather than production, and recreation rather than creation. For Jameson, both postmodernism and postcolonialism are characterized by a compulsion to return to past texts and artefacts through the means of quotation, appropriation, rewriting, and reviewing. Here, Shakespeare can function as the model of a poet and playwright whose plays are objects of cross-cultural reconstructions contrary to the current ideological and sociocultural exigencies of a postmodern/postcolonial era. The reorientation of representations of his canonical plays is manifested in relation to the binary structures of colonizer-colonized, East-West, white-black, male-female, centre-periphery, and also to the deconstructive gaze emerging from within the metropolis itself, spearheaded by Jacques Derrida, Michel Foucault, Richard Rorty, Jean Francois Lyotard, and various others. Their theories on deconstruction and the death of the author are used to undo Western culture's claim to centrality and historical persistence.

This volume is a new contribution to the multiplicity of perceptions about the relationship between postmodernism and postcolonialism. This academic event was an opportunity for the contributors to bring to the fore diverse perspectives related to these two concepts on inherent discursive and aesthetic concerns and on the relationship that reconciles both these movements. The study day also sought to explore the confluences and continuities between both movements in terms of their projects and their conceptions of such notions as history, subjectivity, and representation. One way of comparing the postmodern and the postcolonial entails looking at their discourses and examining their attitudes towards the validity of earlier legitimating (master) narratives of Eurocentric imperialism. Equally important in such a comparison is the shedding of light on the relationship between East and West and the exploration of the ways in which such a relationship is presented and re-represented in a multitude of forms in postmodern and postcolonial writings and re-writings of literary and cultural works from the past.

The present volume brilliantly addresses all of these issues.

CHAPTER ONE

AN ANALYSIS OF HYPERREALITY IN PAUL AUSTER'S FICTION (AARIFA KHANUM, PHD SCHOLAR, LPU)

The postmodern individual, according to Jean Baudrillard, lives in "the desert of the real." (Simulacra 1), which is a place in which there is no longer any reality in its purest form. This is due to the fact that the unending production of counterfeits signifies the demise of reality and truth., which in turn leads to the emergence of hyperreality. The objective of this study is to investigate the many ways in which hyperreality might be examined in Paul Auster's *Moon Palace* (1989) and to argue that it is possible to find a path out of hyperreality. According to the findings of this study, the lack of reality is due to a skewed and piecemeal understanding of historicity, which arises from the fact that current individuals are unable to establish any kind of connection with the past. Therefore, the void of rootlessness has a tendency to be filled by a shallow and imitative present that resembles pop-art imagery created in the manner of Andy Warhol. Every postmodern subject, when placed in a cosmos like this one, where there is no space for any type of divergence, ends up being exactly the same as the millions of others, but by themselves. As a result, the ordinary and prosaic situation of the current world finally develops the world of hyperreality, which is a world in which , it would seem, everything is more engaging and less parched than the so-called "desert of the real" outside. On the other hand, it is hypothesized that the postmodern individual gets sick of the obvious artificiality of hyperreality and seeks to rediscover the real in order to avoid the barren wasteland of both meaning and reality that is abandoned by their lack of connection to the real world. This assertion is made within the context of this research project.

Paul Auster's book *Moon Palace* was released in 1989. The protagonist of the story, Marco Stanley Fogg, is the book's narrator, and he lives in New York City. He is an orphan, whose mother dies while he is a child, and whose father never appears in the narrative. As a result, only Uncle Victor is able to provide for him. When Fogg's uncle suddenly dies, he begins reading the books that his uncle gave him before he died, and the story continues from there. "That was how I chose to mourn my Uncle Victor. One by one, I would open every box, and one by one I would read every book" (Auster 21).

As a result, Mr. Fogg has a secure haven in his collection of books, of which there are over a thousand in total. Fogg withdraws within himself as a hermit in grief at the death of his uncle. Uncle Victor's novels become his bread and butter as he struggles to make ends meet. Fogg is forced to leave his flat since he has no more books to sell and is low on money. Fogg runs into Kitty Wu just as he's about to leave his apartment, and she and an old acquaintance of his named Zimmer rush to his aid when he's in the worst of shape in Central Park. Fogg and Kitty eventually fall in love as he regains his full fitness. Fogg obtains a job reading to a blind man named Thomas Effing in order to make ends meet. Fogg and Effing's pasts become clearer to Fogg over time. Fogg receives Effing's money and moves in with Kitty Wu after her death. They split up when Kitty tells them she wants an abortion. Solomon Barber, who happens to be Effing's son, joins Fogg on a journey to Utah, where he intends to learn more about Effing's background. Due to an accident in a cemetery where Fogg's mother is buried, Barber dies and forces Fogg to continue the voyage on his own. In the end, Fogg walks west till he reaches the Pacific Ocean and this is how the story concludes.

As the above summary shows, *Moon Palace* is a novel with a lot going on, which makes it nearly impossible to sum up. Only the most important things in the book are mentioned above. Even though there aren't that many characters in the book, the strangest things happen to the ones that are there. Also, these events are either the result or the cause of other events, which makes it hard to figure out what happened and why. *Moon Palace* has been looked at from many different angles.

To begin, Fogg is an orphan, which separates him from history and transforms him into a "rootless" postmodern person who does not have any connection to any other grandnarrative or to history itself. Because he is "Emily's love child," (Auster 4) his mother passes away when he is a youngster, and both before and after his mother's passing, his father is "all a blank" (Auster 4) for him. The only thing that his mother says about his father is that "he died a long time ago,"... "before you were [was] born." (Auster 4).Because of this, Fogg decides to accept the narrative that his father was "a space traveler who had passed into the fourth dimension and could not find his way back." (Auster 4). According to Hutcheon, "we only have access to the past today through its traces – its documents, the testimony of witnesses, and other archival materials." (Hutcheon, *The Politics* 58). Hutcheon contends that our sense of the past is built via our encounters with its many representations.

A connection of a similar kind may be seen between the past and the present in the suit that Fogg acquires from his uncle Victor and that he decides to wear for a period as if it were armor. According to Fogg, anytime he was feeling lonely or down, he would always: "swadd[ling] in the warmth of my [his] uncle's clothes provided him refuge and comfort and he adds that there were even times when he believed that the suit was actually holding me [him] together" (Auster 14-15) He even says that he was afraid that, without the suit, "my body would fly apart" (Auster 14-15). So, at first, Fogg's life was organized around the suit, just like it was with the books. But it doesn't take long for the suit to wear out and be "gone" (Auster 25), which breaks the connection to the real world and the past again.

Fogg is also forced to wear Effing's late buddy Pavel Shum's coat in addition to Uncle Victor's clothing. "Mrs. Hume was ordered to fetch the coat that had once belonged to Pavel Shum. ... That was how I came to inherit my predecessor's overcoat. ... I had been turned into Pavel Shum's ghost" (Auster 116). Fogg's comment implies that the two jackets were an effort to establish a connection to the past. They did, however, finally "turn him into a ghost," which distanced Fogg from the world and from himself.

As Baudrillard says in "*The Ecstasy of Communication*," the hyperreal has even crept into our homes. This is because we live in a time in which there is "forced extroversion of all interiority" and "forced injection of all exteriority."

"But today it is the very space of habitation that is conceived as both receiver and distributor, as the space of both reception and operations, the control screen and terminal which as such may be endowed with telematic power that is, with the capability of regulating everything from a distance, including work in the home and, of course, consumption, play, social relations and leisure. Simulators of leisure or of vacations in the home like flight simulators for airplane pilots become conceivable. Here we are far from the living-room and close to science fiction". (Baudrillard, "*The Ecstasy of Communication*" 128)

According to Jean Baudrillard, the house has become a virtual representation of the actual world. Consumption, interpersonal relationships, and leisure activities are all being simulated in this "virtual environment". It is true that his theory relies heavily on TV and media, yet in Fogg's instance the hyperreal arises even without these influences; Rather than try to integrate himself into society outside of his apartment building, Fogg develops his own hyperreal theory of the universe based on his lack of desire to "fit in" (Auster 15). As a result, for him, the world he perceives within his apartment is superior to the reality outside. Although Fogg was with Uncle Victor, he says he and Uncle Victor would establish hypothetical kingdoms and "overturn the laws of nature" in this game they played (Auster 6). For both Fogg and Uncle Victor, "it probably made sense that we should want to leave the real world as often as possible because of the challenges it had produced for them" (Auster 6). Fogg's selfnihilation, like this tiny game, gives a drift from the modern world to his own hyperreal. As a result, he now encounters a manufactured, ambiguous, and repressive reality there.

"Today, it is the real that has become the alibi of the model, in a world controlled by the principle of simulation. And, paradoxically, it is the real that has become our true Utopia - but a Utopia that is no longer in the realm of the possible, that can only be dreamt of as one would dream of a lost object". (Baudrillard, Simulacra 122-23)

According to Jean Baudrillard's theory, the real has been replaced by the model, making it impossible to get the real. This New York apartment's books, suit, and predetermined life of Fogg all serve as templates for a replication of Fogg's journey through life. Even if they erase his previous existence, they become "more real than the real" because "it is simulation that is effective, never the real" (Baudrillard, Simulacra 56). As a result, for Fogg, everything outside the apartment complex becomes non-existent, meaningless and superfluous. For example, Fogg is aware that there are various fellowship programs available for someone in his position; nevertheless, after thinking about it, he decides that he dislikes the concept of attempting to be a member of society; so, he joins his own. Fogg admits that there is no chance for him in the outside world. The moment of realization was so profound that he made up his decision to never aid himself again; refusing "even to lift a finger" (Auster 20). "Human beings have disappeared" from the age of simulation, says Baudrillard (Baudrillard "*On Disappearance*" 24). Fogg's "DIY escape" techniques (Bauman, xviii) include of entering entire simulation, therefore his self-nihilation might be seen as such a vanishing. Inside access the hyperreal, Fogg must first leave his apartment building, which confines him to the confines of the hyperreal, rather than attempt an outside escape. As a result, Fogg puts himself in a position where he has little hope of finding purpose or explanation in the hyperreal world he has created. "When everything is repressed, nothing is anymore" (Baudrillard, Simulacra 147), he opens the doors to everything by detaching himself from everything. A lack of real-world reference points leads in a profusion of meanings and realities that have no real-world counterparts. Consequently, there is no genuine to be replaced and no fake to be substituted. Hyperreality obliterates both of these concepts in a single blow. Only pictures or illusions exist; "behind" images there are additional images; there is no moment at which the ultimate illusion is torn away to reveal... reality (Pawlett, Jean Baudrillard 71). It's much like the layers of an onion: each layer turns out to be empty and meaningless. When Fogg enters hyperreality, he has this experience. Fogg transforms into a clone of himself in this strange new world. It's as though "the subject is itself and never resembles itself again," which haunts it like a subtle and always avoided death (Baudrillard, Simulacra 95). This means that Fogg takes a vacation from his self-image, which leaves him without a reference point in the novel's last chapter. This imaginary world Fogg has constructed for himself in his apartment building is neither a fantasy nor a nightmare. Since Fogg's arrival, the world has become a hyperreal place where everything he sees and feels is both real and unreal at the same time. Since his self-destruction provided the "reality" he sought, he can now call it "reality." A place of refuge from the fractious world that surrounds him.

"The real is produced from miniaturized cells, matrices, and memory banks, models of control - and it can be reproduced an indefinite number of times from these. ... It is no longer anything but operational. In fact, it is no longer really the real, because no imaginary envelops it anymore. It is a hyperreal" .... (Baudrillard, Simulacra 2)

Hyperreality, on the other hand, develops symbols of nonexistent realities. It is a word used to describe the way the universe gets absorbed by one's predilection for illusory items rather than actual ones, according to Torikian (Torikian 100). The apartment life that Fogg has chosen for himself gives him with several instances of hyperreality, in which the perception of reality reaches a level of realism that exceeds that of reality itself.. According to Fogg, "visions of feasts" and "gigantic bowls of fruit" (Auster 28) are only two examples of how his mind is always filled with thoughts about food even when he isn't hungry. He claims that he would see visions from his mind that would emerge and then disappear. Images of Uncle Victor's clothes or even a glass of lemonade, a newspaper with Fogg's name on it, or even his drunken past self searching for anything (Auster 29). "I've also found myself chewing imaginary food, smoking imaginary cigarettes, and blowing imaginary smoke rings into the air around me him ,"he continues (Auster 29). As a result, he argues that these are the hardest times since he "could no longer trust myself himself" (Auster 29). For him, the intensity of his "self-absorption was so intense that he could no longer see things for what they were: objects became thoughts, and every thought was part of the drama being played out inside me him" (Auster 53). Evidence that Fogg has reached the hyperreal, where there is no longer any boundary between the real and the unreal, may be found in moments like this

This period in Fogg's life may be seen as a transition from the second to the third order of simulacra. To hide the fact that reality is missing, the sign claims to be a duplicate of the original, even if there is no original. It's obvious to Fogg that the visions of food and other recollections of his old existence aren't real, that they're only his imagination. In the paragraph presented above, Fogg argues that he may have begun to lose track of the border between the real and the unreal. As a result, his thoughts "had [has] started to drift" (Auster 29). The third step of simulation may be referred to as this phase. During the third stage, when the simulacrum is no longer able to reference any type of reality, the hyperreal takes over. At this point, Fogg is unable to tell the difference between fiction and reality, and he loses faith in the world around him. Thus, Fogg explains, he had to persuade himself that "I [h]e was no longer real" in order to hold himself together (Auster 29). This implies that when we reach the simulation realm, the real and the difference between the real and the fictional are both erased. For example, when Fogg first meets Kitty Wu and her friends over breakfast, he insists that Cyrano and his journey to the moon are true and fiercely rejects the idea that he is a fantasy. Cyrano, he claims, was "a creature of flesh and blood, a real man who lived in the real world, and in 1649 he wrote a book about his trip to the moon" (Auster 37-38). "A genuine guy who lived in the real world," says Fogg of Cyrano. Later, Fogg was too preoccupied with his thoughts to answer the door of a 'real' person who had knocked on his door, and who Fogg left unanswered because he couldn't figure out who would be "that desperate to see me [him]" (Auster 43). Fogg responds to the landlord's criticism that he doesn't have a "decent" work by pointing out that he has a "permanent" job: attempting to "live through another day" (Auster 45).

New York City's Central Park serves as a second hyperreal space for Fogg's imprisonment. Hyperreality may be found beyond the limitations of a restricted space like Central Park. Like everything else in postmodern culture, Belsey thinks, the idea of space is heavily influenced by subjectivity and human awareness (Belsey 3). Because of this, Fogg describes his surreal experience in New York as "this was New York, but it had nothing to do with the New York I had always known" (Auster 54). Central Park's status as a realm of the hyperreal has shifted, and it now serves as both a sanctuary and a shelter from the streets for him (Auster 55), allowing him to clear his vision and seek guidance from within. When Fogg is at Central Park, he is in the most terrible financial situation of his life. Thus, the hyperreal cosmos that he creates around himself in this situation is much more encompassing than the apartment block he is searching for anything to cling on to.

"The process will, rather, be the opposite: it will be to put decentered situations, models of simulation in place and to contrive to give them the feeling of the real, of the banal, of lived experience, to reinvent the real as fiction, precisely because it has disappeared from our life". (Baudrillard, Simulacra 124)

According to Baudrillard, in complete simulation, the model asserts its existence in such a manner that finally the real becomes fiction. Also, when in Central Park, Fogg chose to refer to the trash cans he ate leftovers from as "cylindrical restaurants, pot-luck dinners, municipal care packages" in order to "deflect myself [himself] from saying what they really were" (Auster 59). When he visits a coffee shop or cafe, he likes to select a few toothpicks to create the idea that he had just eaten something to pass the time. This is an example of the real being obliterated by the depiction of the real, much as dining at potluck restaurants and eating with a toothpick when hungry are also instances of this.

With his multiple disguises for different situations, Effing is a character in the book who most questions the idea that reality can be defined. So many characters appear in the book that it's hard to know who the actual Effing is until the very end. "if real is a word that can be used in talking about him [Effing]" (Auster 98). On top of that, he often raises doubts about what constitutes "reality." On one occasion, he inquires of Fogg"'[a]re you sure you're alive, boy? Maybe you just imagine you are.' 'Anything is possible. It could be that you and I are figments, that we're not really here. Yes, I'm willing to accept that as a possibility'" (Auster 102). As a result, Effing is a complete defiance of reality.

Hyperreality may be seen in Effing's descriptions of his time spent in the deserts of Utah.

"The land is too big out there, and after a while it starts to swallow you up. I reached a point when I couldn't take it in anymore. All that bloody silence and emptiness. You try to find your bearings in it, but it's too big, the dimensions are too monstrous, and eventually, I don't know how else to put it, eventually it just stops being there. There's no world, no land, no nothing. It comes down to that, Fogg, in the end it's all a figment. The only place you exist is in your head". (Auster 152)

Effing's experience in the desert of Utah has therefore equipped him with a virtual environment that has eliminated all other possibilities. If they are powerful enough, Effing says, "a man's thoughts can change the world around him" (Auster 101). In the desert, Effing has existed entirely in his brain. Thus, Effing says "[o]nce you've done that, boy, you never forget it. I don't need to go anywhere. The moment I start to think about it, I'm back. That's where I spend most of my time these days— back in the middle of nowhere" (Auster 122) Since Fogg had entered the hyperreal in his own captivity, Effing would do the same. It demonstrates how postmodern people are able to transition between several worlds. He also relates a moment when he assumed the position of a deceased hermit, which he describes in detail.

Effing reasoned that "if anyone came up there to pay him the hermit a visit, he would simply pretend to be someone he was not—and see if he could get away with it" since they were around the same age, Effing assumed (Auster 162-63). This shows that Julian Barber was wiped out by the model and that he would never be re-acquired. According to Effing, the hermit once had a visit from an Indian. The Indian was duped into thinking he was the hermit because of his convincing demeanor. The hermit "was looking for [Tom the hermit], he wasn't about to question who had given it to him. In the end, it was probably a matter of complete indifference to him whether he had been with the real Tom or not" (Auster 170) .Hyperreality and its pictures, as seen in this illustration, have obliterated and replaced reality. A postmodern person only knows what they have seen and not what they are. When it comes to obtaining their desired outcome, They could care less about what the truth has to say. Only the sign can be seen. Like the Indian, who desired to see the hermit and eventually did, the hermit was able to be seen by the Indian.

Additionally, Effing had to plan his meals methodically while living in the cave as a hermit (Auster 165). This encounter is essentially identical to the experiences that Fogg had at the apartment building, yet it is also very different. As a result, reality is once again privatized. Fogg's question "but how do we know there ever was a cave?" is relevant here. Kitty responds, "[o]f course he was telling the truth" ... "His facts might not always have been correct, but he was telling the truth. Even if there wasn't an actual cave, there was the experience of a cave" (Auster 269).As a result, privatization of reality is what Kitty is alluding to. According to Ashvo-Muoz, "in an age of hyper-reality fiction, reality is increasingly displaced by simulacra, showing a crucial concern about credulity. One is aware that there is more than one way to interpret reality." (Ashvo-Muoz 34). As a result, Effing's cave and becoming a recluse became his reality. Regardless of whether or not there was ever a real cave, he lived in it.

To put it another way, Effing is an isolated figure that has no ties to the actual world. In Beville's words, "postmodernism expands to examine the self as alienated from the community and also from itself" (Beville 46). In fact, Effing reveals that Fogg had previously used a "sissy name" that he "always detested" (Auster 125). "Julian Barber" was his real name. As a result, Effing has lost all sense of self and has become a carbon copy of himself. Despite the fact that Thomas Effing lacks creativity, he is more genuine than the long-dead Julian Barber. Since Fogg doesn't know his name, he asks him a question like, "[y]ou can't give someone the name, can you?" (Auster 190). As a result, Julian Barber no longer exists, but its copycat Effing does. Even though Julian Barber may have been a fantastic artist, Effing's paintings were always more perfect. Fogg said this towards the conclusion of the tale. To put it another way, since the hyperreal is "perfect, infinite and more exact in their representation of the real than reality itself," (Auster 226).

Fogg escapes the hyperreal loop while Effing transforms into a simulacrum with the assistance of Zimmer and Kitty Wu. He escapes from his flat and Central Park with the aid of his buddies. As a result, he is allowed to leave. Fogg's critical perspective on his hyperreal experience would not emerge until after his rescue by Kitty Wu and Zimmer. For example, he merely claims that the rescue "alters the reality of what I [he] experienced" after leaving the hyperreal apartment tower (Auster 49). His rescue will allow him to walk out of hyperreality, even for a short period of time, since he will know that there are people who love and care for him, thus he will return to normalcy. As a result of the rescue, Fogg realizes what a horrible state his clarinet, which he had been dragging about the whole time, was in. Fogg didn't notice the clarinet was broken when he found it in Central Park, but it had been there the whole time. Because they don't recognize the difference between living in a simulation and not, postmodern people take the simulation of society/the world for granted. Everything, according to Baudrillard, is a simulation and there is no other reality than hyperreality. For this reason alone, the Moebius strip may be broken, as Fogg was able to do. It didn't take Fogg long to "resemble the person I [he] had once been" after the rescue (Auster 79). It's becoming more difficult for him to maintain close relationships with his friends and family as the book progresses. As a result, towards the novel's conclusion, he finds himself once more alone and cut off from the rest of society. However, by the conclusion of the story, Fogg seems to have given up to the meaninglessness of his sentence and is no longer concerned with whether or not he can transport the rock to the summit of the mountain. To emulate Sisyphus, one must "imagine him happy," as he did (Camus 123).

To conclude, this study examined the postmodern book Moon Palace (1989) by Paul Auster in connection to Jean Baudrillard's idea of hyperreality. This conclusion has been reached by an examination of the novel's characters, who experience hyperreality. It has been suggested that the characters are dragged into hyperreality; yet, with the assistance of those who care about them, they eventually find their way out. However, the world they encounter after leaving hyperreality is devoid of purpose and significance. Therefore, people are left looking with their eyes wide open into the nothingness of postmodern civilization.

Works cited

Auster, Paul. Moon Palace. Faber and Faber, 1989.

Ashvo-Muñoz, Alira. "Aura; Ontological Materiality of Existence and Fabulation." *Analecta Husserliana: The Yearbook of Phenomenological Research, Volume IC: Existence, Historical Fabulation, Destiny*, edited by Anna-Teresa Tymieniecka, Springer Netherlands, 2009, pp. 27-35.

Baudrillard, Jean. "The Ecstasy of the Real." *The Anti-Aesthetic: Essays on Postmodern Culture*, edited by Hal Foster, Bay Press, 1983.

---. "*On Disappearance*." Jean Baudrillard: Fatal Theories, edited by David B. Clarke et al., Routledge, 2008

---.*Simulacra and Simulation*. Translated by Sheila Faria Glaser, University of Michigan Press, 1994

Bauman, Zygmunt. *Intimations of Postmodernity*. Routledge, 2003. Behler, Ernst. Irony and the Discourse of Modernity. University of Washington Press, 1990.

Beville, Maria. *Gothic-postmodernism: Voicing the Terrors of Postmodernity*. Edited by D'haen, Theo, and Hans Bertens. Rodopi, 2009.

Belsey, Catherine. *Culture and the Real*: Theorizing Cultural Criticism. Routledge, 2005.

Camus, Albert. *The Myth of Sisyphus*. Translation Edition, Vintage International, 2018

Hutcheon, Linda. *A Poetics of Postmodernism*: History, Theory, Fiction. Routledge, 2003.

Torikian, Garen J. "Against a Perpetuating Fiction: Disentangling Art from Hyperreality." *The Journal of Aesthetic Education*, vol. 44, no. 2, 2010, pp. 100– 10.

CHAPTER TWO

On Capitalism and Technology; A study of Don DeLillo's Cosmopolis (Naphia Akther, Ph.D Research Scholar, LPU)

Technology has changed the way people perceived the world. "The technology...would be the master thrust of cyber-capital, to extend the human experience toward infinity as a medium for corporate growth and investment, for the accumulation of profits and vigorous reinvestment" (*Cosmopolis*, 207). The dominance of technology engenders complete shift in temporality, in which the past and the future collapse in, rendering in the present eternal, which is different from the concept "now". It refers to the limitlessness of time, or timelessness. *Cosmopolis,* DeLillo's solitary novel gave to the depiction of American money related market, enters New York City, the budgetary heart of worldwide capital at the turn of the new thousand years. Technology has changed the manner in which individuals saw the world.

The protagonist reaches the zenith of his power when he is in his car. Packer's limousine operates as a medium where technology and capitalism meet, thus serving as an elaborate tool of power. Packer retrofits the interior with "visual display units" and "medleys of data on every screen, all the flowing symbols and alpine charts" and "a heart monitor" (*Cosmopolis,* 13). It is when Eric engages directly with technology that we see his power and yearning for dominance in full view.

Essentially, technology grants Packer power, and he communicates through technology to manage his staff: "[he] spoke a coded phrase to a signal processor in the partition" which "generated a command on one of the dashboard screens" (*Cosmopolis,* 25). Eric's need for newly updated, faster technology and his craving to know the future attests to his hegemonic views and his insistence on being in power. He believes that ATMs are "anti-futuristic, so cumbrous and mechanical that even the acronym seemed dated" 18 (*Cosmopolis,* 54), and as he drives by the bank he wonders "why cash registers were not confined to display cases in a museum of cash registers in Philadelphia or Zurich" (*Cosmopolis,* 71).

In addition to technology, Eric Packer's career as a global trader influences his inability to connect with others and his posthumanist subjectivity. Rogue capitalism explains Packer's harsh treatment of, and opinions toward, others. He goes on to posit that "[g]reed, social prestige and often obscure forms of psychoemotional gratification serve as catalysts for misconduct of the rogue capitalist," allowing for destruction of society's greatest asset: community and societal harmony. Because the rogue capitalist, in a sense, distances himself from society and his specific community, we can safely call him individualistic, greedy, and, most importantly for this project, someone who lacks empathy and consideration for others. Furthermore, Eric Packer works within the realm of cyber capitalism, or with "'[t]he interaction between technology and capital. The inseparability"(*Cosmopolis,* 23). Packer's missing empathy and attention toward others allows for a buttressing of his posthuman subjectivity; this subjectivity is also rooted in his addiction to technology—thereby to his rogue capitalist ideology—which largely determines his personality and decisions.

In *Cosmopolis*, Eric Parker resides in the eye of financial storm and suffers severe mental stress, incapable of working out a meaning for life. An extravagant way of life is nothing but a reflection of inner anxiety. People carve for material possessions which could have been done without to release the tension from inner world. Eric owned an apartment of forty-eight rooms which he equipped lap pool, card parlor, gymnasium, shark tank and screening room. Speed is undeniably one of the elements posing pressure on people's mental state. He had two private elevators. "One is programmed to play Satie's piano pieces and to move at one-quarter normal speed" (*Cosmopolis*, 29). The reason why he uses the slow elevator which even brings hatred from other people is that it helps settle the unsettled mood.

Ultimately, Parker decides to follow the impulse of having a haircut in the barber's where his late father was also a frequent. Once he starts his journey, collages of public violence are incredibly witnessed from within his white limousine. Self-awareness awakes in a gradual way. But DeLillo does not stop his story at the awaking of Parker's perception of life; he aims to explore more. As an ex-employee of the super capitalist becomes a constant threat to his life, death seems to be the destination of Eric's one-day journey. In this sense, haircut is more like a ritual than a mere impulse---a ritual for an escape of present predicament. But where exactly does the escape lie in? DeLillo embeds an escape in his protagonist's digital existence. Does it suggest that technology provides a solution to people's mental predicament? DeLillo's philosophical thinking tells us the answer is never simple: the end is an end without end. Efforts put to looking for a runaway from modern dilemma eventually turn out to be self-deceptive. The biggest pandemonium on Packer's haircut journey could be the anti-globalization demonstration which is so destructive that it brings about conflicts between demonstrators and the police.

Packer's limousine conveyed him to the hair stylists the place his childhood memory lived. Eric Parker has a versatile office furnished with cutting edge advanced gadgets - his limousine which is reinforcement plated, enriched with marble floors and fitted with cameras empowering him to get a scene from its inside. Be that as it may, we read his internal requiring a common life in the absolute starting point of the story: He archaic business just beginning to stir, produce trucks rolling out of the markets, news trucks out of the loading docks. The bread vans would be crossing the city and a few stray cars out of bedlam weaving down the avenues, speakers pumping heavy sound (*Cosmopolis*, 7).

In *Cosmopolis*, Eric Packer adopts every single item of the latest technology as it appears. His mind is under the influence of technological wonders to the extent that he wants to "live on a disc" (*Cosmopolis*, 105). He is connected to various material things in his life, not only to his gadgets but his other possessions, as well. The first scene introduces Packer as feeling strangely connected to his home – the modern, high-tech building that embodies his values to a significant. This contributes to the way he perceives reality, and thus himself. For him, technology is a way to foresee the future, outgo the present and triumph over it. The technology in his limousine helps him predict the events, thus allowing him to control the flow of cyber-capital.

Technology is a way to work with his capital directly but by using its digital representation. It helps him be completely distant from the physicality of money, yet make it increase in his bank account. It also helps him seem distant and unaffected by the world in chaos brought by the changing conceptions of time and space, as well as of self and reality. As Packer's antagonist in the novel Benno Levin states, Packer is "always ahead, thinking past what is new" (*Cosmopolis*, 152). His ability to see into the future is more a matter of the technology available to him and to a lesser degree a matter of natural gift. Eric Packer is not a prophet; he is an analyst. DeLillo represents him as the man who has mastered technology to the level that he is able to see patterns in reality and make assumptions about the future.

Eric's limousine completely blends into the environment on the outside. However, on the inside, it is highly equipped, enabling Packer to constantly monitor the flow of information, equally concerning the economy and the media. It is a surreal machine, "less an object than an idea" (*Cosmopolis*, 10). With its flat plasma screens and surveillance systems it becomes his whole world – it replaces the office, the bar, the place where he can meet his mistresses. This way it forms a hybrid environment, a surreal and hyperreal cell that traps him inside the world of never-stopping data. He himself is fascinated by this world, mesmerized by the information and completely enchanted by "the hell-bent sprint of numbers and symbols, the fractions, decimals, stylized dollar signs, the streaming release of words, of multinational news, all too fleet to be absorbed" (*Cosmopolis,* 80). However, he fails to recognize that these signs are all there is – they are just the image of reality with no real value in it, other than the abstract value we ascribe to it. The digital representation of capital is a signifier, Baudrillard's simulacrum – an arbitrary construct which might as well be empty of any meaning. This is why Eric works with cyber-capital; on a metaphorical level, DeLillo involves him with a simulacrum and not real, palpable money to highlight the lack of connection between the real world and the image that only claims to be real.

A similarly sharp and philosophical character in *Cosmopolis*, Vija Kinski is absorbed in information and in the world of statistics and she states that they "are not witnessing the flow of information so much as pure spectacle, or information made sacred, ritually unreadable" (*Cosmopolis*, 80). She is much more aware of the true nature of this spectacle, and she often analyzes the media and contemporary society.

The reason for this is, DeLillo seems to suggest, that people rely on technology and the media to tell them what is real and how to behave. The examples such as Jane Melman in *Cosmopolis*, who prefers face to face communication, rather than consulting one of Eric's many screens for information, are rare and even perceived as strange, out of touch with the real world merely for the fact that they are actually out of touch with the hyperreality they inhabit. Moreover, they all constantly seem to perform.

In *Cosmopolis*, the omnipresence of technology and the media directly dictates the lives of Eric Packer and the rest of DeLillo's protagonists. In The Silence, the utter absence of these elements indirectly highlights the level of importance technology and the mass media play in the protagonists' lives. Under the influence of these elements, the shifted perception of the world that DeLillo's protagonists experience is reflected in their identity issues. DeLillo's dystopian America of these two novels directly results in his characters' becoming lost, unsure of themselves and always on a never-ending quest for something real in their lives. All protagonists exhibit complete and unconditional reliance on technology;

Kinski sees the destructive urge as the hallmark of capitalist thought, because old markets must be re-exploited. The temporal division between the old and the new is the arrival of the new millennium. The destruction goes so far that protesters even set off bombs outside the investment bank. *Cosmopolis* portrays a world in which one could become the most powerful investor by quickly establishing a digital finance model. Eric Packer is one of them and he soon has connection with Russian tycoons and even American president. *Cosmopolis* dramatizes the international currency markets that Eric Packer has manipulated to become the most powerful investor on the planet. Capital is the leading stimulation on urban people's mental state and technology is the conspirator. The inseparable two see each other grow with and for the other. Hand in hand, they build up the illusion of capitals. Eric Packer makes his money through international currency exchange. He studies the flow of currency information with the aid of advanced communications technology. The transcendence of real world has induced the obsolescence of time and space when finance gains momentum in accelerated dynamics of instability.

Unlike Benno, Eric has alienated from any real sense of need and has lost touch with the real world. In fact, the world Eric lives is the world of imagined needs and because these needs are imaginary, the commodities that he possesses don't satisfy his real need and have no real purpose. The very instance of it is his "forty-eight room apartment with its lap pool, the card parlor, borzoi pen, the gymnasium, shark tank and screening room and atrium"(*Cosmopolis,* 3).

Packer fully engrosses himself in the global market, resulting in strained and masturbatory relationships with others. The most problematic of these relationships is with his wife, Elise. The unromantic newlyweds struggle to converse, and when they do speak, the conversation creates tension. Elise and Eric's breakfast together early in *Cosmopolis* embodies their relationship. After Elise divulges a secret about her writing process and serious psychological damages from a 19 challenging relationship with her mother, Eric objectifies his mother-in-law. He says, "'I like your mother. You have your mother's breasts...Great standup tits'" (*Cosmopolis,* 18). Through Eric's interactions with Elise, we see the rogue capitalist's absence of empathy for or awareness of his immediate community. Another example of Packer's disconnection from others, especially from women, takes place after he and Jane Melman masturbate and climax together. In a post-climax moment of sensitivity, Jane says to Packer before she leaves the car, "I am advising you in this matter not only as your chief of finance but as a woman who would still be married to her husbands if they had looked at her the way you have looked at me here today" (*Cosmopolis,* 54).

The incessant display of the murder desensitizes viewers, and that desensitization, by extension, makes them lose compassion for others. Packer engages in mediated responses to another murder, this time of Nikolai Kaganovich, a Russian man "of swaggering wealth and shady reputation" (*Cosmopolis,* 81). He and Eric were friends, and although they respected each other, Eric "was glad to see the man dead in the mud. ... Eric felt good about it, seeing him there, unnumbered bullet wounds to the body and head" (*Cosmopolis,* 81-82).

Packer's obvious lack of empathy grounds his ruthlessness and genuine unconcern for others. Important to note is the way in which Packer receives the news that his rivals have died. Eric learns about the murders through the television, which amplifies the distance between him and the rest of the world. He relies solely on technology for information and uses it for clout, intensifying his posthuman subjectivity. Ironically, though, technology also subverts Eric's power. Throughout *Cosmopolis*, Eric's visions of the future come from technology. These prophetic moments perplex Eric whenever they occur. The first time he witnesses a kind of techno-time jump, he questions the functionality of the technology: "Eric watched himself on the oval screen below the spycam, running his thumb along his chinline" as if to ensure that the relationship between the camera's recording and the real-time action are in sync. He asks his data analyst Michael Chin, "'Why am I seeing things that haven't happened yet?' (*Cosmopolis,* 22). Next, while Eric and Jane Melman masturbate together, Eric looks up and see "his face on the screen, eyes closed, mouth framed in a soundless little simian howl" (*Cosmopolis,* 52). These glimpses culminate into Packer's most profound act of foresight when he appears to witness his death.

In the novel's final chapter, Benno Levin, also known as Richard Sheets and one of Packer's disgruntled former employees, corners the protagonist in an abandoned warehouse. Throughout this final scene, Packer sees stages of his death through the screen on his watch. First "[t]here was an image, a face on the crystal, and it was his" (*Cosmopolis,* 204). Then, "the image on the screen was a body ... facedown on the floor" (*Cosmopolis,* 205). Next appears the image of the "inside of an ambulance," and finally Eric sees a tag with "Male Z" written on it: "He knew that Male Z was the designation for the bodies of unidentified men in hospital morgues" (*Cosmopolis,* 206).12 The common denominator in these prophetic scenes is the technology through which Packer espies the future. Consistently, the posthuman protagonist wishes for the fastest technology in order to be more well-informed about his surroundings and the market's movement. This need is a preventative measure: Packer is paranoid about his situation in life.

The displacement of his posthuman condition continues as Packer rides to the Nasdaq Center in the heart of Times Square where the anti-globalization protest occurs. In the middle of the novel, Packer undergoes his first shift in subjectivity during which he realizes how capitalism, specifically rogue capitalism, in an age of globalization functions. For Packer it is a "shift, a break in space" (*Cosmopolis,* 97). This realization occurs when Packer sees the self-immolating man in the middle of the anti-globalization protest. Prior to seeing the burning man, Packer believes that the protest represents "the market culture's innovative brilliance, its ability to shape itself to its own flexible ends, absorbing everything around it" (*Cosmopolis,* 99). After musing on how "[t]he protest was a form of systemic hygiene, purging and lubricating," Packer sees "a man in flames" (*Cosmopolis,* 99) in the middle of the city. And, then, finally, Eric recognizes that the market, the glow of the cyber-capital world, is flawed: "What did this change? Everything, he thought. Kinski had been wrong. The market was not total. It could not claim this man or assimilate his act. Not such starkness and horror. This was a thing outside its reach" (*Cosmopolis,* 99-100). These prophetic moments suggest the fracture of Packer's posthuman subjectivity; they represent Packer's disengagement with time and his fluctuation towards a humanist subjectivity. A motif in DeLillo's work, the immolating man echoes Thích Quảng Đức's famous protest in 1963. References to this event appear in *Players, Mao II, Underworld* and *Zero K*. This act of protest monumentally alters Eric. He is overcome with a need to understand and empathize with the protestor:
Eric wanted to imagine the man's pain, his choice, the abysmal will he'd had to summon. He tried to imagine him in bed, this morning, staring sideways at a wall, thinking his way toward the moment. Did he have to go to a store and buy a box of matches? He imagined a phone call to someone far away, a mother or a lover. (*Cosmopolis,* 98-99)

Conclusion

As in all of DeLillo's works, art and technology work together to depict the contemporary moment. *Cosmopolis* offers us a glimpse of the greed that rogue capitalism engenders and the social and personal ramifications that stem from an obsession with technology. Undeniably abounding in our world, art serves as the key to understanding ourselves and what surrounds us; while Packer does not fail to recognize his faults, it takes a devastating act of protest for him to fully realize the errors of his ways. He, however, continues to return to technology and a posthuman subjectivity until his death. Packer's wavering posthumanist and humanist subjectivity attests to the idea that he represents the twenty first century's battle between technology, capitalism, and art.

Works Cited

Baudrillard, Jean. *Simulacra and simulation.* University of Michigan press, 1994.

Delillo, Don. "Cosmopolis, New York, Scribner, 2003; trad. it." (2003).

Duvall, John. (ed.). (2008). The Cambridge Companion to Don DeLillo. Cambridge: Cambridge University Press.

Mirbabazade, Seyyede Fateme, and Alireza Jafari. "Consumption as Sign in Don DeLillo's Cosmopolis." *International Journal of Applied Linguistics and English Literature* 2.6 (2013): 67-75.

Shelat, Jay. Convergence : The Meeting of Technology and Art in Don Delillo's Cosmopolis and Zero K (2017).

Stamenković, Slađana. "Human Identity in Hyper-Reality: The Hyperreal Self in Don Delillo's Cosmopolis and The Silence." *Belgrade English Language and Literature Studies* 13.1 (2021): 243-264.

Wang, Jun. "Technology and the Predicament of Time in Don DeLillo's Cosmopolis." *Theory and Practice in Language Studies* 8.8 (2018): 1069-1073.

CHAPTER THREE

Towards a New Humanistic Paradigm: A Postcolonial Analysis of Richard Flanagan's Novels (Pooja Kumari, Ph.D Research Scholar, LPU)

Postcolonial Literature is an introduction to surveying issues, themes, debates, and themes in works from American, Asia, Africa, and South America, and other colonized places in the world. It negotiates the ideologies and representations from subverts and Euro-American. In the postcolonial non-European cultures and literatures have been marginalized as the effect of colonial rule, dominance, and atrocities on the natives by the British Empire. This literature seeks to negotiate, understand, and critique particular historical 'event'- colonialism or colonial rule- while looking ahead to a more just, politically and socially egalitarian settings of world. This literature is called as the literature of "resistance, protest, anger and hope". It tries to make us understand the history so as to settle the future. This chapter intends to throw light on colonialism, post colonialism especially highlighting the Australian postcolonial aspects in which Tasmanian colonization has attained a specific attention. Richard Flanagan shines in the galaxy of postcolonial writers like Chinua Achebe, Salman Rushdie, Jean Rhys, Buchi Emecheta. Though Australian postcolonial writers like Henry Lawson, Rolf Bolderwood, Petrick White, and Judith Wright have attained a worldwide attention due to their writings dealing with the subject but Richard Flanagan is perhaps the first to give the "voice to the voiceless" in the wilds of Tasmania to reflect the pathos of the aboriginals through his writings.

The presented study entitled '*Toward a New Humanistic Paradigm: A Postcolonial study of Richard Flanagan's select novels*'is a qualitative content analysis to find out the hidden as well as "ignored" aspect of Tasmania, an island area of Australia located 240 KM to the Australian South mainland separated by Bass strait. In past few decades the colonial history of Australian colonization by British and its political, social, cultural and economic outcomes have raised enough academic attention. This academic interest, especially after the emergence of post-colonial literature, has covered a long way in giving voice to voiceless victims of British colonization, the aboriginals of the land by tracing their culture and history. The "associated Islands" are still fighting for their story of colonization and its subsequent outcomes to get explored (Broome, 21).

The Booker prize winner Richard Flanagan fills this gap in the context of Tasmania when he contextualizes discourse of colonization in his novels. He is one of the finest fiction writers in the literary world who have constructed whole body of literature keeping eye primarily on the colonial discourse of Tasmanian civilization hence contributes in breaking the so called "the great silence of Australia". To discuss such credible but rare voice from an unknown Island is not only worthwhile but also necessary and would be the sole aim of this chapter. This study will explore the trajectories of colonization in five novels of Richard Flanagan that are *The Narrow Road to The Deep North, Gould's Book of Fish, Death of A River Guide, The Sound of One Hand Clapping* and *Wanting*. The chapter will highlight the gradual development of the post-colonial theory and its major contributors with special emphasis on Edward Said's 'Orientalism' and Laura Doyal's 'Inter Imperiality' and explore in detail the postcolonial discourse in the select novels of Richard Flanagan. It highlights the untold story of Tasmanian aboriginals and hence giving voice to the voice less. The theoretical frameworks of two post-colonial thinkers that are Edward Said's "Orientalism" and Laura Doyle's "inter-imperiality" have been employed to explore the discourse of British colonization in all his novels.

Tasmania and British colonization--

Tasmania is an island state of Australia located 150 miles to the South of the Australian mainland. At present its population is around half million. Various geographical studies (Faramtu,27) as well as cultural studies have confirmed that around ten thousand years ago Tasmanian aboriginals had got separated from mainland aboriginals completely because of rise in the sea level. Since then, they had developed their distinct culture and lifestyle. British landed on this island for the first time around 1800. In 1803, Tasmania had become the 'permanent settlement' of British Empire. The 'permanent settlement' (also called as 'penal colony' or 'exile colony') was referred to a geographical area where the criminals and convicts of mainland Britain were used to deported and kept in prison as punishment. Majority of 'permanent settlements' that had created during the era of British colonization in nineteenth century were located in remote locations; usually it would be a colonized island. Within twenty years of its brutal expansion, it (colonialism) turned many exotic islands into the land of convicts (Burns, 16). Tasmania was one of them. According to historical evidences, till 1853, more than a half million convicts were sent to Tasmania. Hence, slowly and systematically, indigenous aboriginals of Tasmania had been reduced to 'secondary population' and British officials and convicts had become the 'primary population' of the island, having all resources of the island at their disposal (Broom, 32). But for indigenous aboriginals the brutality of colonization didn't stop at inflicting 'homelessness' upon them. The mis-governance of British officials had proved havoc for aboriginals. They failed miserably to regulate the tension between Black aboriginals and white convicts, initiated mainly because of the lack of resources in the island like food, territory etc (Shamp, 43). While black aboriginals fought mainly to protect dwindling food supplies and their women and girls, who were being abducted and raped frequently. For white convicts the whole matter was to suppress native threat (Heiss,16). Lack of policing resources on the part of the Colonists, they preferred to stay aloof and to get involved minimally (Pascoe,14) Moreover, in 1826 Governor George Arthur issued a notice declaring that colonists are free to kill aboriginals in self-defense.

Once hostilities were controlled, by 1832, aboriginals were forced by the governor of that time George Augustus Robinson to move to Flinders Island. Because of the poor health condition, unhygienic surroundings and mismanagement of officials lead aboriginal population to decimate further (Grant, 18). In 1800's, when British came to this island for the time the population of aboriginals was around ten thousand. But within forty years of British colonization the aboriginals were completely wiped out. This act of 'genocide' and 'massive ethnic cleansing' in this remote island of Tasmania is still the least explored and told story of British colonization. It's a great Australian silence (Broome, 36). Few of works, we have, which delve into this hidden chapter of colonization comes from handful of histories like Robert Hughes, Tom Lawson and Lyndall Ryan. The dearth of literature on this episode of British colonization is crystal clear. The Richard Flanagan is one of the rare fiction writers from Tasmania who break this 'great Australian silence' by creating the whole body of creative literature (in form of five novels) on the discourse of colonization by keeping Tasmania at the centre of the discourse. Main purpose of this study is to explore the discourse of colonization in the selected works of Richard Flanagan. To explore the aspect two theoretical frameworks of two different theorists of post-colonial theory that are Edward Said's 'Orientalism' and Laura Doyle's 'inter imperiality' have been applied.

Richard Flanagan and his 'new humanistic paradigm'-

Richard Flanagan was born in a remote town of Tasmania in 1961. He is a noteworthy writer who is known for a range of critically acclaimed writings. He is considered as "the finest Australian novelist of his generation." He attended University of Tasmania and Worcester College, Oxford. He began his career with non-fiction works before moving to the fiction. His first non-fiction work is an autobiography of so called "Australia's Con Man" John Friedrich. His first fiction work was his first novel *Death of a River Guide* which was published in 1994. After that he went on to publish six other novels that are *Sound of One Hand Clapping (1997), Gould's Book of Fish: A Novel on Twelve Fish (2001), The Unknown Terrorist (2006), Wanting (2008), The Narrow Road to The Deep North (2013)* and *The First Person (2017).* With this whole creative endeavor, he successfully establishes himself as an Australian writer of international repute. His *The Narrow Road to the Deep North* (2013), which received Man Booker prize in 2014, gave immense push to his reputation as a writer and secured him a place of 'star writer' not only of Australian circle but of the world. At present he is also the ambassador for the Indigenous Literary Foundation.

Except *The Unknown Terrorist* and *The First Person,* all of his other writings in combination engage profoundly with the 'discourse of colonialism' with Tasmania as its centre. To craft this whole discourse of colonialism through various characters and narration Flanagan employs multiple themes in extremely layered manner (Finner 11). The uniqueness of all these themes and frames is that sometimes they agree with each other and sometimes they disagree with each other. But Flanagan employs all of them to design a very layered and nuanced discourse of colonialism. From theoretical perspective Flanagan's myriad themes, which frame his whole discourse of colonialism, can be contextualized with two different concepts of two different post-colonial thinkers that are Edward Said's 'Orientalism' and Laura Doyal's 'Inter-Imperiality'. Although both of these theoretical frameworks almost have contradictory assumptions and starting points, Flanagan skillfully manages to use themes of both of these frameworks in constructing his discourse of Colonialism to voice to the voiceless aborigines of Tasmania and hence is striving for a new humanistic paradigm in postcolonial studies.

Post-Colonial Theory: Edward Said's 'Orientalism' and Laura Doyle's 'Inter-imperiality-

Before getting into the post-colonial theory generally and into Edward Said's 'Orientalism' and Laura Doyle's 'inter-imperiality' and the utility of these theoretical frameworks for my research work particularly, let me begin with a brief history of colonialism. The traces of colonialism go back to the European explosion of industrialization in 14th-15th century. The industrialization had pushed the production capacity of European countries to multiple times. They needed new consumers and new markets to keep fueling their industrialization, which was bringing them huge profits. Despite of many other reasons, this was the major driving force behind the whole philosophy of colonialism. Ernest Renan is the first scholar who gave intellectual foundation to the wings of colonialism though his book *Intellectual and Moral Reform* (1871). He argues that some races are superior to other. It is moral and ethical duty of superior race to civilize the beings of the rest of the world. Later on, myriad explanations-sociological, political, economics, philosophical, historical, cultural, religious- had been given to justify the conquests of so called "colonial masters". It was mainly after the 2nd world war and subsequent economic decline of European powers, the "rise of third world" occurred. Except nation building, the major focus of these newly independent countries was to produce "post-colonial literature" to counter all above stated colonial narratives. This period saw the rise of so-called post-colonial theory.

Post-Colonial Theory or as generally known as "Post Colonialism" is a rigorous academic endeavor to investigates the impact of colonialism and imperialism across the globe. It traces historical, social, political, economic, philosophical, and cultural legacy of colonialism at various geographical sites of the world (Amaru, 24). It draws theoretical nuances from multiple theoretical paradigms like critical theory, post modernism and post structuralism (Young,47). Notable theoreticians from myriad academic backgrounds like Frantz Fanon, Edward Said, Gayatri Spivak, Homi K Bhabha, Dipesh Chakrabarty, Amar Acheraiou etc. have contributed significantly in building a robust theoretical paradigm of post colonialism. No doubt that today post-colonial theory has developed a rainbow-like theoretical paradigm, preferring investigation of all colonial aspects including literature. It encompasses wide variety of approaches and theoreticians who may not agree on one common set of definition. But there is one foundational bottom line which informs all schools of post colonialism and that is that colonial rulers should not and must not be the only producers of knowledge (Young, 12). Post colonialism more or less look at colonial rulers as 'unreliable narrators. No doubt that colonial rulers have right to produce knowledge as freedom of expression but their narratives must be countered by the knowledge production of indigenous colonized people, whom colonialism has left voiceless after hundred years of rule. So, to understand the colonial life better with the perspective of colonized people must be taken into account.

Theoretically this research work will be governed by the Edward Said's theory of Orientalism and Laura Doyle's theory of Inter-imperiality. Although both of these theoretical stand points are contradictory to each, as I will discuss it further, both of them are equally important to grasp the Richard Flanagan's concept of colonialism with all its complexities. Edward Said is considered as 'the originator of post-colonial theory' because of his so called 'first seminal contribution' in this field in the form book named *Orientalism* (1978). For Said, Orientalism is a grand unethical endeavor of European colonists to construct cultural, social, political, historical, economic, and political identity of their colonized inhabitants in such way that it will justify the project of colonization and hence related brutalities and oppression (Said, 29). And in this process Europe divide the whole world into two 'social constructs', a kind of Us -and -Them boundary that are 'Occident' and 'Orient'.

During the era colonialism in eighteenth century, the 'occident' or the 'West', which consider itself culturally and intellectual superior has created the cultural and social concept of backward, uneducated and uncivilized 'East' or 'Orient'. In this us-and-them orient paradigm European scholars represent the 'Orient world' as inferior, backward, irrational and wild in comparison to superior, progressive, rational and civil occident world (Said, 37) This cultural division of whole world into two social categories, according to Said, allowed Europeans to unleash their colonialism, hence oppression and suppression across colonies in Middle East, Indian subcontinent and Africa. He further elaborates this thesis in *Culture and Imperialism (1993)* and discusses in detail the relationship between power and knowledge. He argues that construction of "African" or "Indian" identity in western literature is actually a colonial form of power. The story of Australian aboriginals is also not much different and they were also the victim of this "identity construction" by European colonizers. The entire industry of intellectuality, consciously and unconsciously, was dedicated to this work. As he mentioned in this book that 'all corners of intellectuality are dedicated to this mission- philology (the study of history of languages), lexicography (dictionary making), history, biology, political and economic theory, novel writing and lyric poetry'.

To him the only rebuttal to this identity construction is to present the real picture of indigenous identity and this endeavor can perfectly be accomplished by indigenous writers by narrating indigenous life stories with the touch of autobiographical individualism (Said 44).

This theoretical stand point of Edward Said's Orientalism analyzes the nature and quality of two major types of narratives in Richard Flanagan's discourse of colonialism as portrayed in his selected works- first, the narrative of 'West's brutality on the East' in the wake of colonization. This narrative is one of the dominating narratives in Flanagan's discourse of Tasmania's colonization. Flanagan establishes this narrative mainly by using the discourse of Tasmanian aboriginality. The bottom line of this narrative revolves around the British's colonization of Tasmanian Island in beginning of eighteenth century and subsequent annihilation of indigenous aboriginal. This major narrative is also supported by one sub narrative of 'ecological destruction' during colonization, the issue which is very close to Flanagan's heart. The pain and suffering of exclusion and discrimination of main character Gould in *Gould's book of fish* has been designed by Flanagan in such a manner that it would become a constant reminder of brutality of British colonialism on Tasmanian aboriginals. In similar fashion the character of Mathinna in *wanting* expresses the brutal nature of British colonialism in specific and European colonialism in general. Through the memories of the main character of *Death of A River Guide,* Aljaz, when story runs into flashback, the same narrative of British colonization has been portrayed by Flanagan. The second factor is of 'identity construction' of East by West as uncivil, barbaric and irrational. Through various characters in his novels Flanagan portrays British's biased understanding regarding indigenous aboriginals of Tasmania. The colonizers depicted them as barbaric community which had no control on their passions and to 'civilize them' is the noble cause which had to be done by colonizers. At various level, through various characters in *Gould's Book of Fish, Wanting* and *The Narrow Road To The Deep North* Flanagan not only lay bares the prejudices of European colonizers regarding aboriginals but also seriously questions their civility too. If the Gould of *Gould's Book of Fish* is considered as animalistic and barbaric by his 'White' companions, the other aboriginal character of Mathinna in *Wanting* tells us the same story.

The other post-colonial theoretical aspect is of Laura Doyle's 'inter-imperiality'. This theory of 'inter- imperiality' was first introduced by Doyle in her research paper *Inter-Imperiality: Dialectics in a Postcolonial World History* published in *International Journal of Post-Colonial Studies* in 2007. She went on to develop this theory in detail in her book *Inter-Imperiality: The long Dialectic of Power and Culture*. Her theory has been considered as a seminal contribution in the post-colonial theory. Her theory stands in complete contrast with Said's Orientalism. She challenges the simplified binary of West and East which was central to Said's theoretical understanding. Hence, she challenges the simplistic narrative of colonialism that is West's brutality on East. Instead, she proposes an 'inter-imperial' way of understanding colonization. She argues that instead of understanding eighteenth century European colonization as an 'isolated event' it must be understood in the larger context of 'trans- continental interactions of political and economic fields of several empires operating simultaneously in ancient and medieval period and their relation to capital formation' (Doyal, 22). As she argues that 'the theory of inter-imperiality highlight dialectics in the material, the political and the cultural fields, which pre-date and prepare western European states' entry into an Afro-Asian world system. The first impact in understanding European colonization in such broader perspective of 'inter-imperiality' will be on the concept of power. Rather than focusing on uni-directional use of power from West to East as in the case of Said, she favors 'uneven and dynamic long term multi directional interactions' which lead to the formation of a complex web of power dynamics. Hence, it blurs the clear-cut boundary of oppressor and oppressed the colonizer and colonized. This is what she called 'fluid positionality' in which both elite as well as non-elite switch places between these two categories and there is no right demarcation (Doyal 41).

This theoretical framework will analyze the quality and nature of two kinds of narratives in Richard Flanagan novels. Many characters especially in *The Narrow Road to The Deep North, The Sound of One Hand Clapping* and *Death of A River Guide* have continuous movements across various geographical locations through various cultures, as story moves on. These cross cultures relation has been used by Flanagan many times to undermine the rigid East- West continental boundary of Orientalism. Dorrigo, the main character of *The Narrow Road to The Deep North,* exhibits an 'inter imperial consciousness'. He born in England (British Empire) and then first moved to Syria (Caliph Empire) before finally moves to Australia (British Empire) but later on captured by Japanese imperial forces as Prisoner of War. Same is the story of two major 'White' characters in *The Sound of One Hand Clapping* that are Sojna and her husband who were born in Syria and moved to Germany who later on tried to escape by caught by Nazi officials but somehow managed to flee to Tasmania. The complex power dynamics among characters in which there is no rigid boundary between oppressor and oppressed or colonizer and colonized. At various places especially in *Wanting, Gould's book of fish* and *The Sound of One Hand Clapping* have challenged Orientalism's simplified narrative of power between East and West in which West is always an oppressor and East is always an oppressed. Despite of being a 'White' Australian, Dorrigo, the main character of *The Narrow Road to The Deep North* has to confront brutality of imperialism as prisoner of War in Japanese Jail. In similar fashion all the characters in *The Sound of One Hand Clapping* including Sojna have to bear heavy brutality of imperialism.

The long painful struggle and tragic death of the main character, Aljaz in *Death of A River Guide* is also falls into this same category. Both these theoretical frameworks that are Edward Said's Orientalism and Laura Doyal's Inter Imperiality will be used to analyze the above stated narratives of Richard Flanagan novels to explore his discourse of colonialism. In his all selected novels combination of various tropes of Orientalism and Inter imperiality has been used in various forms.

His first novel *Death of A River Guide* (1994) is a story of a river guide named Aljaz Cosini. In the construction of the overall narrative of this novel Flanagan uses multiple themes of both frameworks of 'Orientalism' and 'Inter imperiality'. The author narrates the story of a river guide who after an unfortunate incident, trapped somewhere in between rocks underneath a waterfall: "He feels himself tumbled by water, then suddenly slammed to a halt, feels rocks frap round his hips and his chest like tightening vices. Feels the water that was for a few seconds benign change its character immediately to that of a mad, rushing sadist, forcing his head and body forward and down and under. And he knows this moment has been a long time coming" (Flanagan1994). Now, at this point when he is just few steps away from his death, his own whole life is flashing before his eyes. Richard has designed the narration of this flash back in such a manner that it uses various tropes of 'Orientalism' as well as 'Inter imperiality'. First and one of the strongest themes of 'Orientalism' of this novel comes in the very beginning of the story.

But he also employs 'inter imperiality' through this character of Aljaz to show how yesterday's oppressor can possibly be turned into today's oppressed and hence blurring the rigid boundary of oppressor and oppressed. This is the perfect trope of Inter imperiality he employs in this part of the story. As story opens, we come to know that Aljaz's ancestors were also among those who inflicted brutality on Aboriginals. But then Flanagan moves on to depict miserable life which Aljaz used lived in contemporary society which at last ends with his painful death. Now, as I explained above, at the beginning of the story we come to know that even his ancestors do not like aboriginals and considered them wild. But Flanagan portrays his present situation in such a painful way that reader starts feeling sympathy for him. Hence, while using the trope of 'Inter imperiality' Flanagan tries to blur the boundary between victim and oppressor.

In his Booker Prize winning novel, *The Narrow Road to The Deep North (2013)* Richard meticulously portrays the pain of an Australian Prisoner of War (POW) who were captured by Japanese forces during second World War. In this novel Flanagan employs the framework of 'inter imperiality' with highest intensity in comparison to his all-other novels.

The whole plot of this novel is in itself is 'Inter imperial' in the sense that one, it situates with in multiple empires: some were rising (Japan and America) and others are falling (Britain) Two, here the oppressor is East (Japan) and the oppressed is West (White Australians). This book mainly revolves around a character named Dorrigo Evans and, "Dorrigo Evans' journey to the Line passed through a POW camp in the Javanese highlands, where, as a colonel he had ended up second-in-command, of one thousand imprisoned soldiers, mostly Australians" (Flanagan 229). It is a multi-layered novel which touches upon the individual as well as societal aspects of a character. As story opens, we realize that Evans has been grappling with a mental dilemma. Personally, he considers himself as morally bad and failed person but the society considers him as hero who survived World War two. He struggles a lot to manage his dilemma. This novel brilliantly deals with multiple themes. The most explicit theme is of negative consequences of war and sufferings of a POW.

Although post war Australian society respects Dorrigo a lot, but he has no respect for himself. He considers himself as a morally bad person. The major reason for this is that he has an affair despite of the fact that he is married to a woman named Ella. He loves Ella because she loves him unconditionally and he values her feelings: "He would live in hell, because love is that also" (Flanagan 447). He finds her company pleasing and shares his feelings with her comfortably. He discloses his pain with her and she listens him: "She so thoroughly believed in Dorrigo and Dorrigo's life that she repeated his opinions as if they were her own, and she did it in a way that always frustrated him" (Flanagan 387). Now here again Flanagan employs 'Inter imperial' structure to portray a white Australian army person in a pity situation who actually worked indirectly for British forces, which was history the most brutal western power of colonization: "The war, though. Everything's different now. It dissolves everything, this war, though. You never saw such things before the war. Did you"? (Flasnagan 299). So here again he subverts the clear-cut boundary of West as absolute oppressor and East as absolute Oppressed as envisaged by 'Orientalism'.

Flanagan has also presented the mental state of Japanese officers who have to deal with prisoners on daily basis. Here again Flanagan tries to challenge simplified narrative of power as explained in 'Orientalism'. In the war camp, "As Dorrigo Evans bowed his head and stepped away from the flames, Jimmy Bigelow stepped forward, shook his bugle to dislodge whatever scorpions or centripedes might have taken shelter there, and raised it to his lips. His mouth was a mess, the palate having shed its skin in rags. His lips had swollen up as well, and his tongue- so swollen and so sore that rice tasted like hot grapeshot." (Flanagan 246).

Richard Flanagan's next novel is *Gould's Book of Fish (2001)*. This is Flanagan's best novel if you want to study various tropes of Said's Orientalism. The main character of this novel is William Buelow Gould. This is the story of self-discovery of this main character. As story begins, we come to know that Gould is very unfortunate since his childhood. Being an aboriginal, he suffered a lot. He grows up as an orphan child. He struggles very hard to feed himself and he faces extreme poverty. Because of the lack of food availability, he is physically weak and is not capable of doing any heavy physical work. Flanagan designs the story of this character in such as way that for reader it becomes the constant reminder of European colonization of Tasmania and the brutal annihilation of indigenous aboriginals and hence employing one of the strongest themes of 'Orientalism'.

As story moves on Flanagan employs other trope of 'Orientalism' that is 'identity construction'. As story moves, we come to know that white men think of him as uncivil and barbaric because of his aboriginal background. This always frustrates him and he could never become the part of present society. He always wants to avoid people to because he is fearful for his identity now. He never thinks of doing any specific job. But because of various circumstances he gets into the artistic business of painting. He never thought, even in his remote imagination, to become a painter but destiny throws this opportunity at him. He comes in contact with Jean Babeuf Audubon who is a painter of birds. Gould starts a business venture with her in the field of painting. He goes on with this business without much thought. Eventually, he becomes famous as an artist in the society. Because of his popularity in artistic circle, he is employed by a prison doctor.

After three chapters, Flanagan introduces a new character that is Tobias Lempriere. Through this character Flanagan introduces one other frame of 'Orientalism'. Tobiais a very ambitious struggling painter who desperately wants to become the fellow of Royal society. When he comes to know about Gould he analyzes all the creative art produced by him and his mind is blown by Gould's creativity. Tobias offers heavy amount to Gould and asks him to work for him. Once Gould says no to his offer, he employs various other unethical means to influence him. Tobias as a character is completely an ambitious man and he thinks that only thing which matters in life is wealth and fame and everyone should be insanely rational enough to pursue these goals without getting trapped into any kind of emotions. He asserts, "When forging money, I had always salved my conscience by concluding that I was merely extending the life of commerce" (Flanagan2001). Through this character Flanagan beautifully depicts the nature of Western colonialism, fueled by the ideas of Enlightenment and severe rationality, which only aims at material success at any cost.

His next fascinating novel is *Wanting (2008)*. Flanagan calls this novel as "meditation of desire". This novel is one of the best novels of Flanagan written largely within the framework 'Orientalism', though at some places it also uses various themes of 'inter-imperiality'. This whole novel navigates between two parallel stories. The time and context of these two stories are completely different yet they are interlinked in a larger post-colonial context. One story is of the greatest writer of English literature, Charles Dickens and the time line of this story is around 18th century in London. The other story is of a young, charming girl Mathinna. The timeline of this story is around 19th century in the Island of Tasmania. British authorities come here to establish their colony on this beautiful island to make political and financial profits. And they find it as their sole aim to refine and polish the natives of Tasmania thinking themselves members of superior race. Being stuffed with the feeling and complex of superiority Franklinres decide to adopt Mathina for making her civilized.

On one morning of 1854 in London, a lady named Jane Franklin visits Charles Dickens. This is the time when Charles Dickens is at the peak of his popularity. He has just finished his great novel *Hard Times*. Jane shares her problem with Dickens. About 10 years ago his husband, who was a pole explorer, had disappeared in his expedition to Arctic pole with his crew member. Since then, the British government has sent many rescue missions but of no avail. Finally, British government has decaled them missing and dead. But now one of the renowned magazines of London has published a story about Jane Franklin's husband that after the few months of their expedition he and his crew member resorted to cannibalism. The magazine's article criticizes his husband vehemently as a head of the expedition. Jean wants Charles Dickens to write an article to counter the claims of this article. Even Dickens gets angry on the irresponsible behavior of the magazine's editing group. He thinks people like Jean's husband are national heroes and they should be respected and admired for their courage. So, Dickens launches a strong counter attack against the facts and arguments of the magazine. While doing so Dickens sounds completely racist. In the defense of Jean's husband, he argues that all the allegations against any such white man does not make any sense because it is morally and ethically impossible for a white man to descend to such level of savages like aboriginals. Because, Dickens argues, white man is civilized enough to control his passion and emotions. Through the thinking pattern of Dickens, Flanagan tries to portray the so-called Western understanding of aboriginal people and hence the whole project of western intelligentsia to construct Eastern identity as devil, as envisaged by Said in his thesis of 'Orientlaism'.

Simultaneously with the above story, Flanagan also narrates the story of a girl Mathinna. White narrating this story also Flanagan employs various frameworks of Orientlaism and mainly of 'identity construction of East by West'. Mathinna is an unfortunate aboriginal girl who born in Tasmanian island. Since her childhood she faces sever situations. But her life improves suddenly when she is adopted by the governor of one of the provinces of Tasmania. She is very dear to the Governor and his wife. But as story unfolds, we come to know that her life has not sorted out yet. One night while Mathinna is sleeping, the governor rapes her. He rapes her very brutally to satisfy his lust.

> "*He was all things and all things were him. Looking down on Mathina, her diminutive body, her exposed black ankles, her dirty little feet, the suggestively of her red dress between her thin legs, Sir John felt thrilled. And after, was thrilled no more" (Flanagan 152).*"

later on, abandon her once he gets transfer orders. Mathinna life becomes worse again. Sever poverty; alcohol and prostitution follow her life afterwards. Throughout this whole story of Mathinna, Flanagan shows that how various white characters around her continuously tries to construct her identity in various ways, hence employing the theme of identity construction of 'Orientalism'. Some of them consider her uncivilized, irrational and barbaric.

Flanagan has also employed this powerful framework of 'Orientlaism' while narrating the horrors of British colonialism through his characters. This novel is the clear depiction of social, political, economic, cultural and psychological damage done by European colonial masters to the Tasmanian indigenous aboriginal people. Flanagan uses Charles Dickens's anecdote just to depict the racist hangover of white people, who believe that white people are superior to other breeds of humans and it is their duty to civilize the world's population. The Mathinna's story is a medium uses by author to investigate the brutal nature of colonialism. As author portrays that the colonialism has not only destroyed indigenous aboriginal culture physically but also morally and most importantly physiologically.

Conclusion:

All above stated descriptions of these novels help us to understand the overall discourse of colonialism from the perspective of post-colonial theories of Edward Said (Orientalism) and Laura Doyal (Inter Imperiality) in the novels of Man Booker Prize winner Richard Flanagan. This chapter would be a new study that provides increased knowledge about Tasmania's discourse of colonization in the literary aspect as well as in societal level. This study helps in finding the scope of implementing the post-colonial literary theory in other works of fiction related to aboriginality. It also facilitates the further studies based on post-colonial literary theory.

Works Cited:

Flanagan, Richards. *The Narrow Road to the Deep North*. Random House, 2013.

............*Gould's Book of Fish*. Macmillan, 2001.

.............*Death of a River Guide*. MacPhee Gribble, 1994

............*The Sound of One hand Clapping*. Pan Macmillan, 1997

..........*The Unknown Terrorist*. Picadore, 2006.

.........*Wanting*. Knoph, 2008

..........*First Person*. Penguin, 2018.

Altman, Jon (1987). Hunter-gatherers today: an Aboriginal economy in north Australia. *Australian Institute of Aboriginal Studies*, 8(3), www.indiginousaboriginalstudies.com

Altman, Jon & Hinkson, Melinda (2009). Coercive Reconciliation: Stabilize, Normalize, Exit Aboriginal Australia. *Cultural Studies Review*, 15(2), Arena Publications, Melbourne: Australia.

Armitage, Andrew (2017) *Comparing the policy of Aboriginal Assimilation: Australia, Canada and New Zeland*. UBC press, Vancouver, Canada.

Attwood, Bain (2009). Power, knowledge and Aboriginals. *Journal of Australian Studies*, 16(35), 1-16, DOI: 10.1080/144430

Bhabha, Homi. (2004). *The Location of Culture*. Psychology Press, New York.

Bennett, Bruce (2008). Of spies and terrorist: Australian fiction after 9/11. *Asiatic*, 9(11), https://journals.iium.edu.

Chakrabarty, Dipesh (2006). *Provincializing Europe*. Princeton University Press, New York.

Davis, Stephen & Prescott, John (2015). Aboriginal frontiers and boundaries in Australia. 8(3), *Aboriginal Studies*, Melbourne University Publication, www.institutionalhead.com

Dixon, Robert (2018). *Richard Flanagan: The critical essays*. Sydney University Press, Sydney.

Doyle, Laura (2007). Inter- Imperiality: Dialectics in Postcolonial World History, *International Journal of Postcolonial Studies*, 16(2).

Doyle, Laura (2012). *Inter-Imperiality: The Long Dialectics of Power and Culture*. NewYork University Press, New York.

Douard, John (2008). Sex Offender as Scapegoat: The monstrous other within. *Heinonline*, 24(7), https://heinonline.org

Free, David. (2009). Missing the point: The prose of Richard Flanagan. *Quadrant*, 53(6), https://search.informit.com

Gayathri P S and Rani PL (2015). Analysis of narrow road to the deep north. *Transnational Literature*, 8(1), http://fhrc.flinders.edu.au/transnational/home.htm

Gittins, Barry and Vuk, Jan (2014). Richard Flanagan sorts suffering from virtue, *Eureka Street*, 24(22), www.jstore.com

Head, Lesley (2000). *Second Nature: The history and implications of Australia as Aboriginal landscape*. Syracuse University Press. New York.

Holgate, BD (2010). Greening a narrative mode: Antipodean Magical Realism and Eco criticism in Richard Flanagan's Fiction, *Comparative Literature and Culture*, 13(4), 43-58, Sydney University Press.

Kampmark, Natasha (2015). Richard Flanagan's The Narrow Road to the Deep North, *Antipode*, 29(2), 486-488, DOI: 10.13110/antipodes.29.2.0486

Keen, Ian (1988). *Being Black. Aboriginal Culture in "settled" Australia*. Aboriginal Studies Press, Canberra: Australia.

Kendon, Adam (2013). *Sign languages of Aboriginal Australia: Cultural, Semiotics and Communicative Perspectives*, Cambridge University Press. London.

Lang, Steven. (2007). Slumming it, *Overland*, 16(4), 18-22, https://search.informit.com.au/documentSummary;dn=200704430;res=IELAPA;type=pdf

Lis Ewa (2014). *Reflections on/of Dickens*. Cambridge Scholars Publishing. London.

Messahel, Salhia. (2009). Richard Flanagan "Post-Post" and the mapping of Alter modern, *Alpine*, 19(6),www.jstore.com.

Plisiewicz, Paul (2009). The distance between desire and need. *Antipodes*, 23(2), https://search.informit.com

Reynolds, Henry (2008). *Other Side of the Frontier: Aboriginal resistance to the European invasion of Australia*. UNSW Press, Sydney.

Said, Edward (1978). *Orientalism: Western Conceptions of the Orient*. Pantheon Books, London. Said, Edward (1993). *Culture and Imperialism*, Chatto & Windus, New York.

Tharoor, Shashi (2017). *Inglorious Empire*. Aleph Book Company, India.

Trigger, David (2004). *White fellas are coming*. Cambridge University Press. Cambridge.

White, Laura. (2006). Spatial Anxieties: Tourists, settlers and Tasmania's effective economies of belonging in A Terrible Beauty, Death of a River Guide and Gould's Book of Fish, *Critical Essay*,https://books.google.co.in/books?hl=en&lr=&ide

CHAPTER FOUR

A STUDY OF TECHNOLOGY AND TIME IN DON DELILLO'S COSMOPOLIS (AGRITA CHIBBER, PH.D RESEARCH SCHOLAR, LPU)

Cosmopolis by Don DeLillo is significant in many ways as it records DeLillo's reaction to 9/11 attacks. It was composed advance, so in this sense, DeLillo's investigation's prophetic idea cannot be disregarded. Unlike another prophetic novel, Mao II, which has already been translated as an expectation of the rise of fundamentalist fear-based oppression that occurs inside contemporary reality, Cosmopolis is prophetic in that it reveals a startling connection between time and creativity. DeLillo distributed an article titled "In the Ruins of the Future: Reflections on Terror and Loss in the Shadow of September" in December 2001, not long after the 9/11 attacks, presenting a brief picture of the nation's transforming bewilderment. "It is the glossy polish of our modernity," he writes. "It is the impetus of our technological advancements... It is the power of American culture to penetrate every wall, every home, life, and mind." (33) Following the events of September 11th, 2001, America is confronted with a perplexing mix of Don DeLillo's most horrific issues. He composes the physical uprooting of tens of thousands of New Yorkers and the spiritual dislocation of a significant number of Americans; he composes the prophetically disastrous fear and neurosis that has been restored. In this era of global finance, worldwide fear-based oppression, and cutting-edge innovation, the relationship between technology and time plays a critical role.

Cosmopolis is the only novel by DeLillo that throws light on New York City and money related market. The story recounts about the protagonist Eric Packer who is a millionaire. He is a money dealer in Wall Street. One fine day he settles on a choice to get hairstyle done. The cross-town path from Eric's opulent home near the UN headquarters to the abandoned distribution centre on the eleventh road was strewn with brutality and deliberate displays of psychological torment. Novel typifies mercilessness and triviality into single day and accentuates that in the age of electronic capital, "we need a new theory of time" (86).

Cosmopolis is divided into four sections with two inter chapters in between. Packer's extravagant triplex is the starting point for the representation. He begins his approach to acquire a hair style after boarding his limousine. However, the common goal becomes a journey that is repeatedly hampered by planned gatherings and encounters. The constant differences in Eric's vehicle's characters follow an execution of current capital breakdown, and no matter what they do, these characters have the ability to remind Eric of an impending future. The seemingly random presence of figures such as his executive of innovation, his supervisor money officer, and so on has a cumulative effect. Minor inaccuracies accumulate throughout the novel's plot and build to a climax.

The key reason for the necessity for "a new philosophy of time" is that innovation and capital are in cahoots, which unavoidably leads to the bind of time that clears now and reality itself. Underneath the way "We die every day" (45), there is a fundamental ontological discernment: we are our own invalidation, destined for nihilism and passing. The breakdown of the money-related market, for example, demonstrates how a quick shift, rather than a slow one, has overturned all the review standards and ideal models and taken control of every picture of our lives. "The inextricability of technology and capital interaction" (23).

Technology has changed the way in which an ordinary person viewed the world, "The technology...would be the master thrust of cyber-capital, to extend the human experience toward infinity as a medium for corporate growth and investment, for the accumulation of profits and vigorous reinvestment" (207). The innovation incites temporariness, in which past and future have broken down, giving present the unending power. It is similar to the idea of endlessness that is not bound to end. In DeLillo's novel *Zero K* the concept of agelessness is given. DeLillo cites Herbert's poem "Report from the Besieged City" (2007) as a prophetically catastrophic representation of things to come at the entryway of another thousand years. In Herbert's poem "I" was assigned to make a chronological record of a war-torn and then abandoned city. I decided to write in the rhythm of weeks: "Monday: stores are empty a rat is now the unit of currency" (416).

In the novel Cosmopolis, 'rats' are substituted with various monetary issues and is connected with mindless money related issues or markets. It reverberates, "specter haunting the world...the specter of capitalism" (96). The haunting is not so much a figment of the past but an anticipation of the inevitable commodification of whatever emerges in the real world" (Martina,2015). Cash has the power to make time, cash has lost its story quality that means it cannot follow past or in future.

Eric Packer the main character of Cosmopolis, is totally dependent upon money and goes through a lot of pressure. Luxurious lifestyle is just an impression that shows internal nervousness. Individuals sacrifice for material possessions that may have been managed without releasing the stress from within. Eric owned an apartment with 48 rooms, including a lap pool, a poker parlour, a gym, a shark tank, and a screening room. Time is definitely one of the variables that have an impact on people's mental health. He had two personal elevators. "One is programmed to play Satie's piano pieces and to move at one-quarter normal speed" (29). The motivation behind why he utilizes the moderate lift which even brings disdain from other individuals is that it helps settle the agitated state of mind.

Finally, Packer chooses to follow his desire of acquiring a hairstyle at the hairdresser's where his late father used to go. From inside his white limousine, he sees unfathomable collections of open viciousness when he starts his journey. Mindfulness gradually emerges. Regardless, DeLillo''s story does not end with Packer's awakening to a new perspective on life; he intends to delve further. Eric's one-day venture appears to be to kill an ex-representative of the greedy industrialist, who has become a constant threat to his life.

The most uproar on Packer's hairstyle journey may be the anti-globalization demonstration, which is so disruptive that it results in conflicts between demonstrators and police. Because previous markets must be misused again, Kinski sees ruinous desire as an indication of entrepreneur mind set. The landing of the new thousand years is the worldwide division between the old and the new. Nonconformists even detonated bombs outside the venture bank as part of the devastation.

Cosmopolis shows a world where money is everything. Eric Packer is one of the financial specialists and has links with Russian and American President. Cosmopolis demonstrates money advertisers that Eric Packer has taken control of. Capital is the primary motivator for urban residents' psychological well-being and inventiveness. I am the plotter. The indistinguishable two watch each other grow alongside and for each other. They work together to realize the capitalist dream. Eric Packer makes money from the worldwide cash market. With the help of cutting-edge correspondences innovation, he considers the stream of cash data. When account picks up force in hurried elements of flimsiness, the greatness of the genuine world has sparked the oldness of existence. The historically inaccurate nature of time overwhelms the protagonists with a sense of futility.

Time is becoming a corporate asset. It is a product of the free market system. The moment is more difficult to get by... The future becomes increasingly insistent. As a result, something will happen shortly, perhaps even today. To adjust time's acceleration. Return nature to a more or less normal state (79).

The entire work, which condenses a series of spectacular events into a single day, depicts the result of modern life's rising speed. It resembles an orchestra with a fast pace, capturing hilarity and anxiety in the fully promoted time.

The beginning of *Cosmopolis* depicted by DeLillo, “I started out simply with the idea of letting my protagonist drive across town in one day, a person who is already living in the future and fails to notice how susceptible he is to the destructive mechanisms of the present” (Gourley, 2013, p.38). The novel shows how future has taken upon the present through the protagonist Eric Packer. His car Limo is the spotlight of the novel, it is not just a car but a work environment,

“There were medleys of data on every screen, all the flowing symbols and alpine charts, the polychrome numbers pulsing” (13).

However, the past keeps casting its shadow on the present scenario of Packer. Eric’s car limousine dropped him to the hair dresser where as a child he visited with his father. Packer’s current life is a dramatic contrast to the banal conventional though acceptable family story. His brief respite of comfort and peace counteracts the chaos of the day. Cosmopolis genuinely narrates an account of one-day exertion to address over-quickened time, justifying some scrutiny with James Joyce’s *Ulysses*. Eric Packer has a varied workplace with cutting-edge modern equipment - his limousine, which is armoured, has marble floors, and is equipped with cameras that allow him to capture a scenario from inside. Be that as it may, we read his internal requiring a common life in the absolute starting point of the story:

He archaic business just beginning to stir, produce trucks rolling out of the markets, news trucks out of the loading docks. The bread vans would be crossing the city and a few stray cars out of bedlam weaving down the avenues, speakers pumping heavy sound (7).

The protagonist’s ideal existence did not revolve around large sums of money or social extroverted high-class parties. His traditional familial basis masked a desire for a less regimented existence. Memory or the nostalgia from the past in any case, did not protect him from emotional anguish. Packer walked away from the hairstyle and returned to the chaos of life. In light of the lunacy of the capital market, his rise to become a money-related monster was also a sign of medium-term wealth.

Endeavors put to searching for a runaway from current problem in the long run end up being self-tricky. Similarly, as written toward the finish of the novel, “He is dead inside the crystal of his watch but still alive in original space, waiting for the shot to sound.” “The interaction between technology and capital the inseparability” (23). With the urbanization of private enterprise, urban individuals are confined in the wild and stinging pressure deep down, and apparently. The strain fundamentally becomes out of mechanical advancement and capital globalization. The efforts to try to find a way out of a current situation end up being self-tricky in the long run. “He is dead inside the crystal of his watch yet still alive in original space, waiting for the shot to sound,” as written at the end of the story. “The inextricability of technology and capital interaction” (23).

It (technology) convinces us that we must live eternally in the future, amid the utopian light of cyber-capital,” DeLillo writes before September 11, “Because there is no memory there, and everything is faster, better, greater, yet simultaneously shapeless, low in height, and transitory" (Gourley 39). Individuals’ conceptions of time have altered in today’s highly competitive culture. Individuals were formerly free of time constraints, and as the twentieth century progressed, people began to describe efforts to break free from the shackles of conventional time in writing by researching mental time. To laymen maxing out of time, innovation could be a vital component. Money nowadays buys time. Previously, it was the other way around, but now the things have changed drastically.

However, these changes have made the internal a weak and fragile. Internal uneasiness therefore weakens language, which invariably analyses an individual’s relationship with the world. Eric, like Oswald in Libra, is a hero who is overwhelmed by unfathomable truth since he has no one to trust. The rule is quietness. Individuals are influenced by their own uneasiness to ignore other people’s looks, even eye contact. Eric only occasionally exchanges eye contact with those around him. Torval looked at Eric when he responded to Eric’s inescapable threat of attack, which “seemed like a tremendous violation, defying the logic of coded glances, voice tones, and other gestural boundaries of their particular terms of reference” (102).

Eric Packer faces a turmoil that throws him in a pool of confusion. He faces psychological issue where he starts doubting his true self. The history maker during the capital era, who should have been on the opposing side of the protests, did not feel threatened or surprised by what he witnessed. He “decided to admire this” unexpectedly (88). “Did he envy them? The shatterproof windows showed hairline fractures and maybe he thought he’d like to be out there, mangling and smashing" (92). Eric epitomizes the struggle to break the pen of existence in search of opportunity, or if possible, eternal time.

Unrest in the masses should also be taken into account. It reveals more about people's amusement with the choppy nature of the financial market and the control of computerized innovation. Individuals are discovered engaged in displaying, disorder, savagery, and expressing an interest in equality while failing to recognize what they require. Eric experienced the power of globalization, "saw people running, the vanguard of a crowd, coming this way, and others spilling off the sidewalks, startled and confused, and a Styrofoam rat twenty feet tall dodging taxis in the street." (86).

'Terror', DeLillo says, "is now the world narrative, unquestionably." It is also a work of death in DeLillo's books: Arthur Rapp, the IMF's chief executive, was assassinated in Nike North Korea; Brutha Fez, the band's most popular vocalist, died of heart failure; and Nikolai Kaganovich, his prior partner, was shot dead shortly after returning from a walk to Albania Online. Whatever the case may be, Packer appears to be near death. Benno Levin shot him and he died,

He wanted to be buried in his nuclear bomber, his Blackjack A. Not buried but cremated, conflagrated, but buried as well. He wanted to be solarized. He wanted the plane flown by remote control with his embalmed body aboard, suit, tie and turban, and the bodies of his dead dogs, his tall silky Russian wolfhounds, reaching maximum altitude and levelling at supersonic dash speed and then sent plunging into the sand, fire balled one and all, leaving a work of art, scorched earth art that would interact with the desert... (209).

There is a study made by DeLillo on the personal life and his response to it. Eric finally found love, something he had been missing for a long time. The newlyweds spoke in a clumsy and half-magical manner, despite being married but living apart. Eric encountered his significant other Elise Shifrin several times over the one-day journey, which was filled with a kaleidoscope of hilarious events. He thought Elise was "a dangerous person" and that the ballads she wrote were "shit." The thought process of Eric's wedding her was seen as strange as a result of the artist spouse's monster property. It seems to be "Two great fortunes. Like one of the great arranged marriages of old empire Europe" (26). Eric definitely realised his enthusiasm for his significant other as the movement neared its finish, notably when he met Elise for the third time amid a hilarious film production. "I wanted to talk to her, tell her she was lovely, lie and cheat on her, live with her in moderate matrimony, holding dinner parties and inquiring what the doctor said," he says as the story draws to a close (206). Sadly, Elise went without a trace, and love has not been able to help him get out of his mental state.

After he was dead, Eric was stripped of his social identities in the funeral home and returned to the very same reality he had when he first arrived on the planet— "Male Z," which denotes a complete departure from the highly visible life and return to a natural state. "He'd always wanted to be become quantum dust, transcending his body mass, the soft tissue over the bones, the muscle and fat. "The idea was to live outside the given limits, in a chip, on a disk, as data, in whirl, in radiant spin, a consciousness saved from void" (206). Whatever the case may be, there is no one-size-fits-all solution to getting out of the vacuum.

A burst of energies and forces exists within the staleness of temporality. The language complexity between *Body Artist* and *Cosmopolis* is a striking precedent: the former, as DeLillo's first novel after 2000, has begun to pass on a signal of development in his time reasoning. *Cosmopolis* was published at a critical juncture in the history of money, innovation, and legislation. Future intrudes on the present, but also enters the past, and what has occurred evolves into what the future predicts.

DeLillo's writing, as a significant modern author, reflects the shift in time perception in the transforming picture of history. Expounding on DeLillo's fiction after 2000 does not imply a haphazard examination of an author's work.

Works Cited

Boxall, Peter. (2003). Don DeLillo: The Possibility of Fiction.New York: Routledge.

Boxall, Peter. (2013). Twenty-First-Century Fiction. Cambridge: Cambridge University Press.

DeLillo, Don. Cosmopolis. New York: Scribner.

Don DeLillo. (2001). In the Ruins of the Future: Reflections on Terror and Loss in the Shadow of September. Harper's.September 2001, pp. 33-40.

Duvall, John. (ed.). (2008). The Cambridge Companion to Don DeLillo. Cambridge: Cambridge University Press.

Gourley, James. (2013). Terrorism and Temporality in the Works of Thomas Pynchon and Don DeLillo. New York and London: Bloomsbury Publishing Plc.

Glen, Thomas. (1997). History, Biography and Narrative. Twentieth Century Literature, 43, pp.107-124.

Herman, David. (ed). (2007). The Cambridge Companion to Narrative. Cambridge: Cambridge University Press.

Herbert, Zeigniew. (2007). The Collected Poems 1956-1998. New York: HarperCollins Publishers.

Kavadlo, Jesse. (2004). Don DeLillo: Balance at the Edge of Belief. New York: Peter Lang.

Sciolino, Martina. (2015). The Contemporary American Novel as World Literature: The Neoliberal

Antihero in Don DeLillo's Cosmopolis. Texas Studies in Literature and Language, 57, pp.210-241.

Meyerhoff, Hans. (1955). Time in Literature. Berkeley, Los Angeles and London: California Press.

CHAPTER FIVE

Displacement of Minds: A Psychological and Bhabhain Analysis of J. M. Coetzee's Disgrace (Anoop S.R. & Dr. Ghanshyam Pal, LPU)

J M Coetzee is one of the pillars of Post-Colonial English fiction who has carved a niche for himself in the decorated 20th century post –colonial fiction. Transcending the boundaries of region, race and time his novels have received worldwide acclaim and acceptance. His 1999 novel *Disgrace* brought him much laurels including his second Man Booker prize and played a pivotal role in securing him the Nobel Prize for literature in the year 2003. The Swedish Academy in its Nobel prize announcement calls Coetzee a writer "who in innumerable guises portrays the surprising involvement of the outsider." (Swedish Academy, 2003). This statement is particularly true for *Disgrace*, a powerful novel set in the post-apartheid South Africa where the social conditions and the power structures have undergone a paradigm shift.

Disgrace deals with the fall from grace of a well-respected University Professor David Lurie who by his own actions and due to the prevailing hostile social environment ends up being a social outcast. The narrative travels through the landscape of South Africa which is a reflection of the mental travails of its protagonist who is displaced from his position of power, grace and authority to a peripheral role where his existence is not of any importance to the society. In the first part of the novel, Lurie is shown as a Professor in the University of Cape Town, a man in his fifties leading a monotonous mundane life and teaching the same course to student year after year which is primarily about the Romantic poets. To escape from his boredom and tedious schedule he contemplates composing a chamber opera which he likes to call "Byron in Italy" which deals with the times of Lord Byron and his final mistress Teresa in Italy. Though he is socially well respected he has another face in which he appears as a womanizer and a man who is craving for the fulfillment of his sexual desires secretly. He has an ongoing relationship with a prostitute Soraya whom he visits on Thursdays. "For a man of his age, fifty-two, divorced, he has, to his mind solved the problem of sex rather well" (1). But this statement appears to be a vain proclamation from Lurie as the novel progresses his sexual life becomes complicated and goes beyond his control. He engages in an uneasy sexual affair with his student Melanie Isaacs whom he calls the "dark one". Though Melanie does not particularly approve of the sexual advances of Lurie towards her, she mostly remains a mute spectator as Lurie imposes his sexual self over her and engages in sexual intercourse in a rather forced manner. Shocked and devastated Melanie files a sexual harassment complaint against Lurie with the University authorities. As the trail is going on, Lurie pleads guilty of the crime and decides to step down from his post in the University. But he rejects the instruction from the University that he has to offer a public statement of remorse and acceptance of the punishment and leaves for the countryside where his daughter from the first marriage Lucy is staying.

Lurie starts staying with Lucy and initially finds comfort in the new surroundings where he finds himself in. Lucy is running a kennel and engaged in farming and Lurie offers to help her. He gets introduced to Petrus, a black man "the dog man" who helps Lucy with the gardening and kennel and to Bev who runs an animal welfare clinic in which Lurie signs up as a volunteer later. However, as days pass Lurie gets apprehensive of the safety of Lucy as he fears the neighborhood is not safe for a white young woman. His worst fears come true one afternoon as three black men barges into their home- shoots the dogs, incapacitates Lurie and rapes Lucy. Heartbroken and grief-stricken Lurie wants Lucy to file a complaint with the law enforcing authorities but to his surprise she declines to do so. Disillusioned, Lurie confronts Petrus as he thinks Petrus is somehow involved in the whole act of vandalism and rape. But Petrus brushes him aside as insignificant and not worthy of deserving a proper answer. Later Lurie realizes that one of the attackers belongs to Petrus' family and finds him attending a party in home. Lucy informs him that she is pregnant as a result of the rape and that she intends to keep the child despite Lurie's protestations. Petrus offers to marry Lucy and provide her safety and security in exchange of her property and farm which Lucy accepts strangely. Lurie vehemently opposes this idea but Lucy is adamant. She makes it clear that she cannot stay with Petrus and Lurie in the same house and Lurie is forced to move out. Instead of going back to the city he rents a place in the neighborhood and starts staying there. He grows fond of his work in the animal shelter and by now he has learned to give the dogs "love" (219). But as one of the final acts in the novel he brings his favourite dog to the table to put it down to sleep making Bev ask him, "I thought you would save him for another week?" (220) to which he calmly replies, "No, I am giving him up" (220).

Though the story is set in Post-Colonial and Post-apartheid era the psychological elements are scattered all through the narrative. Lurie is a middle-aged man and his fear of loneliness, aging and death constitutes what Maliheh Hushidari calls the "midlife crisis" which leads to the irrational and arrogant behavior of Lurie (Hushidari 8). The term was coined by the Canadian psycho analyst Elliott Jaques and received worldwide acceptance over the last decades of the twentieth century through the book *Passages – Predictable Crises of Adult Life* written by Gail Sheehy. In his subconscious mind he realizes that the prime years of his life is beyond him now and slowly he is approaching the twilight of his life.

> "*Then one day it all ended. Without warning his powers fled. Glances that once would have responded to his slid over, past, through him. Overnight he became a ghost. If he wanted a woman, he had to learn to pursue her; often, in one way or another to buy her" (7).*"

But as a man of pride and self-grandeur he is not willing to accept the fact and attempts to evade it by engaging in acts which are fitting neither his age nor his social stature. Visiting prostitutes, forcing himself sexually over his own student and not willing to issue a public apology he is trying to tide over the fact that he is no longer the charming young man for whom the world was the limit. He misses a female companion with whom he can be happy, comfortable and who can bring some sort of balance to his life. In more ways than one, Lurie's reluctance to accept the fact that the times and society has changed shows a psychological aspect which is a reflection of his aversion to changes and inability to cede his position of authority and power which he considers is naturally owed to him by the society. In an attempt to escape from this midlife crisis, he ventures to compose a chamber opera on Byron. His mind and body are at cross roads mostly in the novel- his body is slowly feeling the pinches of getting old but in his mind, he continues to be the man who commands respect and is naturally equipped with all the social privileges enjoyed by the whites in the apartheid era. As an extension of this midlife crisis, he feels insecure in his own abilities within his mind but is too proud to show them openly. He wants to spend more time with Soraya, an evening or even a night, but not the morning after the sexual act when he will be "cold, surly, impatient to be alone" (2) which shows the typical onset of midlife crisis. Instead of accepting and acknowledging the situation, he tries to cling on to his position of power and tries to assert his authority over those whom he comes into contact with –mostly women. Both Soraya and Melanie are to him only subjects to satisfy his sexual greed which on a deeper level is a manifestation of the psychological need of Lurie to project that he is still in charge of both his mind and body and that he is still the same man who is capable of attracting and satisfying women, even those who are much younger to him. He attempts to find happiness in vain – "however, he has not forgotten the last lines of Oedipus: Call no man happy until he is dead" (3).

It is hard to find a modern novel which is not having the elements or the ideas put forth by Sigmund Freud. Freud's controversial yet path breaking theory of Oedipus complex find reflections in the novel. Freud considers that the Oedipus complex typically develops in the phallic stage approximately between the ages of two and six years where the boy's sexual desire for his mother grows and he starts to view his father as a potential hindrance and wants to eliminate the obstacle. In order to prevent this, the boy's feelings towards his mother are to be suppressed – it most often happens through the process where the boy considers his father as a figure whose presence is a threat of castration to him, and is naturally forced to accept him as superior which ultimately results in letting go of his desire for the mother. Called as primal repression by Freud, this process helps in dissolving the tension surrounding the Oedipus complex failing which there will be psychological trouble and pathogenic effect which leaves a scar in the psyche of the person and will lead to irrational actions. In *Disgrace* it is poignant to note that the absence of a "father figure" permeates the novel. Lurie is mostly tight-lipped about his younger days and upbringing, and his only statement of any significance shows clearly the background to his present dilemma.

> "*He himself has no son. His childhood was spent in a family of women. As mother, aunts, sisters fell away, they were replaced in due course by mistresses, wives, a daughter. The company of women made him a lover of women and, to an extent, a womanizer" (7).*"

It appears that he spent his childhood among a family of women and this must be having its effect on his psyche. The absence of a father figure ensures that he is deprived of the chance to undergo the process of primal repression which in turn hampers the development of super ego according to Freud. It has repercussions on his social life also where he is seen as always longing for validation and approval from others especially women, that he is a capable man. Apart from his sexual escapades he is shown as a loner and no mention of friends are found in the course of the novel and he slowly turns into a "moral dinosaur" (89). He proclaims himself that he is not fit for marriage and has a tendency to belittle others without any obvious reasons.

Freud has used the term 'displacement' in his psycho analytic approach to refer to the situation when a person unknowingly shifts or redirects the attention from an unacceptable or dominant target to a relatively acceptable or the one whom he considers a less threatening one. It is a psychological defense mechanism where a person who feels ill-treated and unduly penalized does not have the courage to question the authoritative figure who has caused the situation, instead diverts his frustration to a weaker figure whom he tortures and ill-treats to satisfy his bruised ego. In "Disgrace", Lurie is not subjected to any particular harassment or injustice, but he finds at odds with the society he is living in. His aging body, self-doubts and the monotonous life style makes him frustrated and he attempts to vent it out through his relationship with Soraya initially and then with Melanie. At various stages, it appears that he almost forces himself on both these women without their consent, purely because he knows they are not in a position to resist and cause any harm to him. He acts as if he has the moral superiority over their mind and body only to distance himself from his own inner fears. He wants them to be servile and obedient to him almost always. His impression of the first meeting with Soraya is a case in point.

> "*The first time Soraya received him, she wore vermilion lipstick and heavy eye shadow. Not liking the stickiness of the makeup, he asked her to wipe it off. She obeyed, and has never worn it since. A ready learner, compliant, pliant"(5).*"

This is how he wants his women to be –compliant to his like and fancies. He attempts to dictate terms with both of them and force his own ways on them. The same is his relationship with Lucy and Petrus. In his mind Petrus is the threatening figure who can cause harm to him and his daughter. But he is not strong enough to take on him in the changed social scenario and hence he redirects his fear and urges Lucy to reject Petrus and move out of the place. Ironically Lucy assumes the "mother figure" and Petrus the "father figure" as mentioned earlier. Lurie is unable to stand up to the father figure whom he despises but is not confident enough to take on. He wants to protect his daughter Lucy, but as a displaced mother figure, we can see Oedipus complex again at work here. Lurie's initial reaction after seeing Lucy after a long time is rather strange.

> "*For a moment he does not recognise her. A year has passed, and she has put on weight. Her hips and breasts are now (he searches for the best word) ample. Comfortably barefoot, she comes to greet him, holding her arms wide, embracing him kissing him on the cheek." (58)*"

Lurie instinctively notices the changes in the body of his daughter and appears to care for it more than her show of affection. In the ensuing pages he thinks of her again; "Ample is a kind word for Lucy. Soon she will be positively heavy." (65). The fact that he cannot keep his sexual urges to himself even in the presence of his own daughter. His fear of Petrus is displaced to Lucy but in a way which has concealed sexual undertones. He realizes Lucy still cares for him and is ready to allow him to be with her in the countryside.

Can the psychological elements in *Disgrace* stand on their own aloof from the interplay of variety of post-colonial elements? Most certainly not – that is where Homi Bahbha's theory of mimicry takes centre stage. According to Bahbha mimicry is "one of the most elusive and effective strategies of colonial power and knowledge." (Bhabha 126). This element in post-colonial literature is used to depict the scenario where the members of the colonized country imitate the language, dress, mannerisms and even to some extent the culture of the colonizers. Bhabha argues that mimicry can become unintentionally subversive, even though the colonized during the process of mimicry almost never realizes that he is undermining the pseudo power exercised by the colonizer and that the systems and practices of the colonizers are hollow and can be easily copied. He continues that colonial mimicry is "the desire for a reformed recognizable Other, as a subject of a difference that is almost the same, but not quite". (126). He clarifies that the colonizer wants to improve the Other or the colonized and to make him look and act like himself but still it is being done in such a way that there is still a clear sense of difference. In this way the Other becomes almost like the colonizer but never quite reaches the same level of hegemonic and cultural structures of the society where the colonizer has placed himself. For the mimicry to effectively work, there should be a continued expression of this difference which Bhabha calls ambivalence.

In *Disgrace*, mimicry works at various levels and through various characters ranging from the protagonist Lurie to the black man Petrus who grows in stature as the novel progresses. The insistence of the colonizer during the colonial era that the mimicry should be ambivalent and that the colonized are never on the same level as him, makes the post-colonial situation delicate and complex. In *Disgrace* the post-Apartheid era is depicted where a reversal of roles has happened - where the colonizer or the oppressor is now reduced to the level of marginalized and is subjected to face the consequences of the effect of mimicry enacted by the once colonized people. Instead of being the submissive subjects who harmlessly mimic the colonized, they have become the ones who use the mimicry for their own advantage in gaining power, wealth and social prominence. Petrus was once a labourer for the white people in the apartheid regime, but now he has become a land owner and socially influential figure who can exert his authority over the white people in the area. He achieves this primarily through mimicking the actions of the whites with which he is all familiar during his services with them. Lurie notices Petrus' use of the English language and believes it is a hybridized version and he is not able to decipher whether it is good or bad. During the apartheid regime the whites have promoted the use of English language among the colonized so that they can communicate with them easily to pass on the commands and orders. But it is coming back to bite them as the same language is used as a tool by the colonized to get their revenge. Petrus' use of the hybridized English language is capable of questioning the very authority of the English language. Bhabha's notion of hybridity which he has borrowed from Jacques Derrida indicates that the colonial authority always attempts to connect discourses with other texts in order to facilitate colonial domination through deconstruction of the meanings of the texts. How this deconstruction takes place and how the way of articulation must be changed so that the hybridization of the colonized and colonizer cultures moves to a level beyond the control of the colonizer is found through Petrus' transformation. He has achieved proficiency in English, learnt and applied modern machinery for farming and leads a life style which is reminiscent of the whites during the apartheid era. He is not having any remorse to the tragedy happened to Lucy and rather shows and indifference as if it's a daily affair when Lurie confronts him.

Petrus assumes the moral high ground which was successfully adopted by the whites to ensure that the blacks always remain under their control. He offers to marry Lucy as if it's a humanitarian gesture whereas his original intention is to get her farm and wealth. In this way he is slowly getting into colonial mindset – where the colonizer acts as if he is helping the colonized by giving him language and a reasonable living condition but in reality, is continuing to exploit the colonized both physically and mentally, darning the natural resources and making the colonized believe that this is what is best they can get. The ambivalent nature of the colonized-colonizer relation again comes into limelight here through the Petrus-Lucy relationship. Lucy knows that Petrus is a shrewd black man and probably he is involved indirectly in her rape by the three black men. Still, she accepts his proposal and is willing to let him move in with her to her house expecting safety for her and her unborn child. It appears that she despises and finds him rather threatening and authoritative, but still feels drawn to him bearing in mind the prevailing social conditions and that she needs him to survive in the hostile neighborhood. This love-hate relationship resembles the one which the colonized are having with the colonizer also. Though he is averse to the authority and oppression of the colonizer he is also willing to co –exist with him as long as he gets the basic requirements of existence from the colonizer which he considers as a favour from the colonizer. Lucy shows the same mindset and in a way it's the reverse of the process of mimicry as she has realized the fact that the revenge from the blacks is inevitable and should be accepted as such and she mimics the colonized attitude of accepting it submissively. Rape which has been one of the oppressive tools used in the apartheid regime by the whites is now identified by the blacks as an easy method of plotting and having their revenge. The brutal way in which the three black men rape Lucy and incapacitate Lurie can also be traced as the element of mimicry fully at work. They are reenacting the brutality meted out to the blacks during the apartheid days. Lurie's words to Lucy days after the brutality stand as evidence to this.

> "*It was history speaking through them.... A history of wrong. Think of it that way, if it helps. It may have seemed personal, but it wasn't. It came down from the ancestors." (156)*"

Mimicry is associated with the shifting of the power equations in the society- and in post-Colonial discourse the figures of Self and Other undergoes a complete role reversal in the novel. In the beginning of the novel Lurie is all powerful and well-respected man in the society and he with all his pomp assumes the figure of the Self in the novel. He is the man on the centre, one who can dictate terms and enjoy the privileges which are associated with the position. Early exchanges in the narrative shows that both Soraya and Melanie though belonging to vastly different strata of the society are forced to assume the figure of the Other, who is rendered mute and devoid of any opportunity to express their feelings. The Otherness of both these characters can be associated with their gender too. As is the cliché in any patriarchal society, the women are the ones who are easy targets for subjugation and Lurie is no different. But both these female characters redeem themselves and distance themselves from the Otherness at various stages of the novel. Soraya, despite being a prostitute and denied a meaningful voice for so long manages to look Lurie in the eye and say that she does not intend to entertain him and his eccentricities any longer. When Lurie attempts to make further approaches, she stands her ground and strictly opposes him. In their relationship the Self-Other dichotomy has turned upside down as she assumes the figure of the Self who dictates the terms and is the more confident and assured among the two. Similarly, Melanie is exploited sexually by Lurie again assuming the dominant and privileged role of the Self in their relationship condemning his student to the status of the Other. But like many colonized countries Melanie had enough of the exploitation and oppression that she decides to speak out and lodge the sexual harassment complaint against Lurie. The tables have turned and Melanie has started receiving public support which would never have been there had she kept on suffering in silence. Once the complaint is public and there is outrage against Lurie, she is changed to the Self figure leaving Lurie as the Other in their complex relationship. Lurie cannot face her and even when he finally decides to apologize to Melanie's family, he avoids facing her directly and instead visits her father and apologizes. It is worthwhile to note that in both these cases Lurie has gone into self-destruction mode burning the bridge between him and the other person involved. This happened mainly due to the arrogant, self-centered and autocratic behavior of Lurie which has striking resemblance to the fate of many colonial regimes around the world. The colonial regimes so often meet their nemesis on themselves where their mismanagement of the feelings and anger among the colonized eventually results in the uprooting of their authority which once felt invincible.

The distortion of the Self-Other dichotomy is evident in the characters of Lucy and Petrus also. Lucy, during the apartheid regime was leading a peaceful yet socially respected life in the countryside. But the tremors of the post-apartheid paradigm shift that has afflicted the society has reached there also and her figure of Self is threatened in the wake of the emergence of more confident and powerful blacks who are now targeting the whites in the area. From hapless Other they are moving towards the dominant Self who calls all the shots in a society where the winds of change are blowing fast. Petrus is the classic example of this role reversal – from being a servant engaged in casual labour by the whites he has now become a landlord and even dares to offer to marry Lucy, a white woman whom the blacks were looking with reverence previously. On the other hand, Lucy takes the opposite route where from being the Self figure she is raped, tortured and her authority brought crashing down by the blacks. But the passive almost indifferent way in which she accepts the change in her fate for the worse is typical of many of the Colonizers once the colonial regime is ended. She tends to accept her tragedy as the natural response for the historical oppression and exploitation meted out to the colonized people by the colonizers. She asks hinting at her situation,

> "*What if.......... what if that is the price one has to pay for staying on? Perhaps that is how they look at it; perhaps that is how I should look at it too. They see me as owing something. They see themselves as debt collectors, tax collectors. Why should I be allowed to live without paying?" (158).*"

In a sense Lucy is averse to running away from her problems and shame unlike Lurie who has left the place altogether instead of staying on and fighting to regain his lost reputation. The actions and attitude of Lucy shows the ambivalent nature of the life in post-colonial society where both the erstwhile colonizers and colonized are co-existing and require each other for survival. No matter how they detest each other they should find a way to co-exist and thrive.

The shifting of the centre and the travel to the periphery is another notable theme in Post-Colonial novels and *Disgrace* also showcases this element. Life on the margins and how the marginalized are trying to find a voice to express their hardships find an expression here also. According to Edward W. Said imperialism is defined by "the practice, the theory, and the attitudes of a dominating metropolitan centre ruling a distant territory." (Said 9). How the relation between the centre and the distant territory (which is better known as periphery) undergoes constant change, can be seen from the novel. The idea which was handled in detail by Coetzee in his previous novel *Waiting for the Barbarians* finds further expression here. At the beginning of the novel, Lurie is at the centre of the narrative and is having all the power and authority which is associated with the Central figure. However, he mostly through his own actions is forced towards the periphery which is often associated with the marginalized and colonized people. The shift of the power centre is evident as the narrative goes on – Melanie has managed to come out of her peripheral figure and to fight for justice and pride. Petrus, as pointed out above has left his servile past behind and moves into a central role which offers him more authority and wealth. Historically the story of the people in the periphery do not find a voice in the narratives of popular fiction, however post-Colonialism has brought radical changes to this approach and sets out to tell their stories so that the whole world can know of their travails and sufferings. The centre needs a periphery to exist, rather it is the presence of the periphery which ensures that the power lies with the centre itself. This interdependence on periphery can lead to the downfall of the centre as the periphery can attain the potential to subvert the power structure of the centre. It happens in the relationship between Lurie and Melanie in the novel. Lurie, having placed himself in the symbolic pedestal of the centre takes Melanie and her feelings for granted only to see that his power, social position and in short, his central position is taken away only because Melanie (the peripheral figure) decides to speak out rather than suffer in silence. Lurie has been banished into the margins of the society figuratively and literally as he abandons city life to join his daughter in the country side. The path his life takes him – from being the central figure to the marginal peripheral figure is the story of most of the white people in the post –apartheid South Africa. So, his story assumes historical proportions as it is not simply the tale of a man but a rendering of a universal theme which can hold true for any post-colonial society.

The situation of Lucy differs from Lurie in the sense that despite being a white woman, she had to choose living in the countryside away from her father who is a dominating figure in her life. Lurie is the symbol of the patriarchal society which conveniently banishes its women to the sidelines thus making them the peripheral figures whose presence is necessary for the centre to flourish. Lurie always attempts to interfere in her life choices and decisions under the pretext that it is for her protection. The indirect suggestion that the women are incapable of making decisions of their own and that there is the requirement of a dominant male figure for her to protect her is another aspect of the Centre-periphery relation. But making Lucy break the shackles and look Lurie in the eye and express her feelings, Coetzee's concept of feminism shines through which is surprising since he is a white male author. She is physically abused and destroyed by the black men who rape her and vandalizes her home, but they cannot break her spirit. Lurie is shaken by the terrifying experience and wants to leave the area with Lucy. But she vehemently opposes the idea and wants to stay back and fight her battles on her own. As she undergoes the horrifying experience, she somehow manages to attain the will and inner strength to carry on, to live a dignified life knowing well that she has not done intentional harm to anyone. Slowly she occupies the position of the centre and Lurie still languishes at the periphery unable to find a graceful way to escape his situation. The element of neo racism, where the blacks meet out inhumane treatment to the white people to assert their new found authority is also connected to the centre-periphery discourse and the ensuing marginalization of people. The whites, who were accustomed to being in the Central position in any power equation over decades or even centuries now find themselves staring at the margins where they have found themselves in the post –apartheid era.

Conclusion

No matter how advanced mankind has become through technological advancement and scientific temperament, the human psyche and its mysterious ways of working still offers a constant source of fodder for meaningful analysis. The elements mentioned above are scattered throughout the narrative of *Disgrace*. But can they stand independently and make sense to a reader? Cleverly and carefully interweaving of these elements will only make a work of fiction dealing with such a theme reach the intended levels of understanding by its reader. The psychological elements and the post-colonial narrative is blended in such a way that what the reader see is an amalgamation of all the elements which makes a post-colonial society tick. Being the master craftsman that he is Coetzee has managed to create a fictional world which can be placed as a mirror against any post-colonial society. The unique narrative style ensures that none of these elements jut out from the pages to the reader and offers enough intellectual exercise to them.

Works Cited

Attridge, Derek. *J M Coetzee and the Ethics of Reading- Literature in the Event.* University of Chicago Press, 2005

Bhabha, Homi K. *The Location of Culture.* Routledge, 1994.

Coetzee, John M. *Disgrace.* New York. Penguin Books, 1999

... *Stranger Shores – Essays 1986-1999.*Vintage,2002

... *Waiting for the Barbarians.* RHUK, 2004

Elliott, Jaques. *The Life and Behavior of living Organisms: A General Theory.* Westport. Praeger Publishers Inc,2001

Freud, Sigmund. *The Interpretation of Dreams.* New York. Oxford University Press,2008

Hushidari, Maliheh. *Midlife Crisis or Male Wound? A Psychoanalytical Study of the Protagonist's Behviour as Midlife Crisis.* Soderton. Soderton University College,2007

Said, Edward W. *Culture and Imperialism*, Knopft,1994

Sheehy, Gail. *Passages – Predictable Crises of Adult Life.* New York. Bantam,1977

The Nobel Prize in Literature 2003. NobelPrize.org. URL: https://nobelprize.org/prizes/literature/2003/press-release

CHAPTER SIX

Hermeneutics of Technology: A Study of Thomas Pynchon's The Bleeding Edge (Rehana Akther, Research scholar, LPU)

This chapter highlights that how Pynchon pursues the socio-historical analysis in *Bleeding Edge* (2013) by retorting again to the discursive binary. Since, at the moment he quite referential about the gore and devastating aftermaths of the 9/11 terror attacks and the new machines of post war era effected immensely the mechanized American society at the outset of the third millennium. An effort has been made throughout this novel about the contemporaneous nature of the characters who are all up to surpass the traditional limits that defined the life and death and are being substituted by virtual reality and Baudrillardian simulation and hyper reality and *Bleeding edge* is a glaring experience to experience it.

Bleeding Edge is Pynchon's first effort to depict the collective psychological backlash following the trauma of 9/11. And every literary convention has been put to use to dramatize and reenact the narrative concerns symptomatic of 9/11 era. Bleeding edge is Pynchon's maiden attempt to deliberate upon the post 11 hysteria that made its echoes all around the world and through the mouthpiece of unconventional detective who is technology pro for the unconventional readers to ponder the disintegrated psychosis that the manipulations of the new shifts of post-humanity and post-apocalypse has in our life. Intertextually Pynchon vouchsafes that the post-human humans as hysterically hallucinated, who became vulnerable target to undefined social systems that controls the virtual sitcoms of technology. The protagonist, Jewish fraud-investigator Maxine Tarnow, a quester for epistemology who starts the story with the words "It's the first day in spring 2001," (474) and pushes her to the conundrum, and one year after, when "pear trees have exploded into bloom" (BE 475).

When Pynchon wrote the *Bleeding Edge,* the ideological shifts that mold our present considerations of American society, be it political or psychological has underwent a dramatic change. It was such dramatic changes that make people subject to the new pseudo-haven of simulation and hyper reality and now induced cybernetic web addiction that postmodern man/women are quite dependent about. It has more so become Coleridge's Albatross in the neck

However, within the premise of narration, the protagonist's search becomes a symbolic proclamation of the 60's social upheaval; Maxine's whose narrative seeks after idealistic world whose "social energy" still remains undecided. Later on, with reference to textual outings at the end of *Bleeding Edge*, a peculiar intimation is being found very much between the interfaces of characters such as Gabriel Ice when Maxine points her gun at his face:

> *"It doesn't happen," Ice carefully watching the muzzle". "How's that, Gabe". "I don't die". "There is no scenario where I die". "Batshit fuckin insane", March out the car window. Better hop on in there with your mom, Tallis. Gabe, that's good to hear, "Maxine calm and upbeat, and the reason you don't die?" "Is that you come to your senses". "Start thinking about this on a longer time scale and, most important, walk away." (473)"*

The things that percolated in the mind of Pynchon while writing this novel is the technological overload that was rampant very much into the social fabric of American society that went ahead in co-modifying the very much essence of human liberalism with result the infinite nature of human being went disintegrated and deshelled.

McLuhan's trope of 'self-amputation', as deliberated in his essay "Narcissus as Narcosis," estimates the cost human beings are paying willingly for being the part of information evolution: "Any invention or technology is an extension or self-amputation of our physical bodies, and such extension also demands new ratios or new equilibriums among the other organs and extensions of the body" (49).

Being a physics student, Pynchon's pedagogical aesthetics about the revolution of humans as social being is quite effected and guided upon by the exposure of society to the invasion of scientific inventions and Pynchon's this perspective became a determine factor within the textual fabric of his writing especially in *Bleeding Edge* to ascertain its validity decades later on. More so such a contention is also shared by Brian McHale in cyberpunk fiction which confirmed that scientific realization has made its inroads into the textual narratives of fiction.

Since last few decades technology has advanced to such an extent that post human theory has undergone poststructuralist deconstruction putting liberal humanism at risk. It is such a risk that disintegrated that Cartesian view of human being. Technological investments lead to the genetic, mechanical and cybernetic turnover of modern man.

In *Bleeding edge* Pynchon asserted that how technology is manipulated by coalition government, law enforcement and big capitalism that willingly forces post-humanism to toe the line along the opportunities for freedom which in turn leads to psychological oppression that ends up the individual consciousness into paranoid state. Desubjectifying the individuals are being programmed whose only inputs and outputs are being valued.

Pynchon through the mouthpiece of Maxine pushes the apparatuses of resistance exposes the economic dealings of his protagonists and of readers that are also programmed in compliance with the matrix of global capitalism that is looming large in our society.

Since the polyvalent title of *Bleeding edge* asserts Luddite's notion that, under neo capitalism, state apparatuses willingly opt for the technologies that guarantee exploitative freedom which is being put to panoptic surveillance and regimented at highest possible level. To put it figuratively the title "bleeding edge" refers to what Deep Archer, calls "'bleeding-edge technology . . . Not proven use, high risk, something only early-adoption addicts feel comfortable with'" (78).

Metaphorically speaking the title "bleeding edge" is a luminal space that intermeshes as a space between an object and surrounding space around it. In the novel bleeding edge the things toss against each other thereby minimizing the space once valued turns into pieces and bits, the reality now seems to be what jean Baudrillard speaks simulation and hyperreality to which mankind now is reluctant to live without especially with the onset of the Internet, according to Pepperell, the line drawn between human consciousness and cyberspace has eased off to that extent which lead the technological conundrums bypass the Cartesian nature of human consciousness by cyber sitcoms and dotcoms adding up ending up as psychological amputation by de-subjectifying the unified nature of self that used to be qualitatively tied to what romantics called epiphanies, or spots of time.

Pynchon highlights the invasion of cyberspace while making characters vulnerable to the' epistemological and ontological convulsion who fail to draw a line between real and reel that is being confirmed at the penultimate part of the novel when Maxine spends most of his time logging into Deep Archer when the site has gone awry as the sitcoms site went open to the immense users across the world thereby putting him into virtual landscape of New York with all its glamour in a fashioned way. Maxine visualizes:

> *" she's finding it harder to tell the real NYC from translations like Zigotisopolis . . . as if she keeps getting caught in a vortex taking her each time farther into the virtual world. Certainly, unforeseen in the original business plan, there arises now a possibility that Deep Archer is about to overflow out into the perilous gulf between screen and face (429)."*

Maxine while talking to Eric feels quite disappoint about the technological maneuvers that are quite rampant in the American society. Maxine speculates:

> *"Hangover of Internet", "that it's over", "not the tech bubble, or 11 September, just something fatal in its own history go all along" . . . "every day more lusers than users, keyboards and screens turning into nothing more than portals to Web sites for what the Management wants everybody addicted to, shopping, gaming, jerking off, streaming endless garbage" (432)."*

To the utter frustration of Deep archer while going open source during his visit to Maxine visits finds that:

> *"What was once a train depot is now a Jetsons-era spaceport with all wacky angles, jagged towers in the distance, lenticular enclosures up on stilts, saucer traffic coming and going up in the neon sky. Yuppified duty-free shops, some for offshore brands she doesn't recognize even the font they're written in. Advertising everywhere. On walls, on the clothing and skins of crowd extras, as pop-ups out of the Invisible and into your face (354)."*

Deep Archer is quite disappointed on his becoming extension of commoditized fetish that is being mechanized and susceptible to the commoditized market of capitalism. Rather than seeking refuge from late capitalism, he has become inseparable part of it.

Ernie comments that the word Internet, derived from DARPANET, is fashioned by Defense Department think tanks during the Cold War "'to assure survival of U. S. command and control after a nuclear exchange with the Soviets'" (419). Ernie asserts:

> *"Yep, and your Internet was their invention, its magical convenience that creeps now like a smell through the smallest details of our lives, the shopping, the housework, the homework, the taxes, absorbing our energy, eating up our precious time. And there's no innocence. It was conceived in sin, the worst possible. As it kept growing, it never stopped carrying in its heart a bitter-cold death wishes for the planet, and don't think anything has changed, kid . . . Call it freedom, it's based on control. Everybody connected together, impossible anyone should get lost, ever again. Take the next step, connect it to these cell phones, you've got a total Web of surveillance, inescapable. You remember the comics in the Daily News? Dick Tracy's wrist radio? it'll be everywhere, the rubs will all be begging to wear one, handcuffs of the future. Terrific. What they dream about at the Pentagon, worldwide martial law." (420)"*

The name Zigotisopol is itself significantly omits out the traditional conception of identity and now seems to be fluid and rather transformed into manifold figurations and functions as Ziggy and Otis showcase their volatile identity by becoming one, they are emotional centers and are failures in the ordinary existence embracing the language of commerce and the commodity undermining all the metaphysical solemnities. Therefore, the spiders and bots which Maxine alludes to are computer programmed interfaces of sitcoms that are interlinked and the characters co-opting for this end up becoming inanimate like automata.

Therefore, it is surmised that all the individuals gradually drift into the obtrusive delivery of what Frederic Jameson's fangs of late capitalism, the self and programmed world are constitutionally opaque subject to the dispersed decentered network of libidinal framework bereft of psychical interiority vulnerable to the media experience, trend and fashion and towards the end of the novel Franklin argues: "is necessary is to make materialist attentiveness . . . into a weapon that can be used against the idealized, fuzzy metaphors and the specific, concrete forms of exploitation and dispossession that together constitute capitalism in the age of control (168).

Everything in the above paragraph is suggestive of decomposition with the inclinations of purposiveness of entropy, apparently the freedom the citizens of American society enjoyed within the garb of Internet, was a gore excuse to demystify the freedom of people, it was a sort of thermodynamic surprise. As Eric Outfield asserts, "You'd think when the towers came down it would've been a reset button for the city, the real-estate business, Wall Street, a chance for it all to start over clean. Instead looking at them, worse than before" (387).

Conclusion

Therefore, like the colonial hangovers of Marlovian Heart of Darkness, we do come across the Patriot Act, the oil backlash in Iraq and frauded enlightenment in Afghanistan, Google, Face book, and WhatsApp, Instagram, Tiktok. Pynchon voushafedly asserts that under the veneer of American dream of enlightenment the American society is on the threshold of destruction and therefore by willingly signaling the to the technological backlash that happen to creep up during2001 and 2013, the textual make up of *Bleeding Edge* witnesses this by making references to the runaway androids with fetishtic attraction to simulate humanoid robots. The novel therefore blurs the boundary between fact and fiction and therefore thresholding readers' consciousness which is haunted by the technological and co modified nature of society, a sort of cosmic awareness that could paralyze mind and the body.

Works cited

Benea, Diana. "Post-Postmodernist Sensibility in Thomas Pynchon's *Bleeding Edge*." *British and American Studies*, vol. XXI, 2015, p. 143-151. Print.

Cohen, Joshua. *Book of Numbers*. New York: Random House, 2015. Print.

---. "First Family, Second Life: Thomas Pynchon Goes Online." *Harper's Monthly*, October 2013, p. 99-105. Print.

Cowart, David. *Thomas Pynchon and the Dark Passages of History*. Athens, GA: University of Georgia Press, 2011. Print.

Darlington, Joseph. "Capitalist Mysticism and the Historicizing of 9/11 in Thomas Pynchon's *Bleeding Edge*." *Critique: Studies in Contemporary Fiction*, vol. 57, no. 3, 2016, p. 242-253. Print.

ELIAS, Amy. *Sublime Desire: History and Post-1960s Fiction*. Baltimore, MD: Johns Hopkins University Press, 2001. Print.

Gourley, James. "Twisted Time: Pynchon's 9/11 in *Bleeding Edge*." *Reflecting 9/11: New Narratives in Literature, Television, Film and Theatre*, edited by Arin Keeble, Victoria Bryan, and Heather Pope, Cambridge, UK: Cambridge Scholars Publishing, Print. 2016. Print.

Hassan, Ihab. "Beyond Postmodernism: Toward an Aesthetics of Trust." *A Journal for Greek Letters*, vol. 11, 2003, p. 303-316. Print.

Hutcheon, Linda. *The Poetics of Postmodernism: History, Theory, Fiction*. London: Routledge, 1988. Print.

Hume, Kathryn. *Aggressive Fictions: Reading the Contemporary American Novel*. Ithaca and London: Cornell University Press, 2012. Print.

Luchn, Marsch. *Understanding Media*. Ithaca and London: Cornell University Press, 1988. Print.

Pynchon, Thomas. *Bleeding Edge*. New York: Penguin, 2013. Print.

CHAPTER SEVEN

Analyzing V.S. Naipaul's The Mimic Man through Post-colonial perspective (Dr. Ghanshyam Pal & Dr. Kumar Gaurav, LPU)

V.S. Naipaul is a best-known English novelist of Indian origin. His novels have beautifully described colonial and ex-colonial societies. The present chapter analyses some complex issues like mimicry, post-colonial, decolonization ambivalence, alienation and in-betweenness in the society described in this novel. The primary purpose is to present the post-colonial identity and the indelible wounds of colonialization which the protagonist bears throughout the novel. It is an attempt to study V.S. Naipaul's *The Mimic Men* (1967) through the eyes of some of the well-known postcolonial thinkers like Frantz Fanon, Homi K. Bhabha, and Edward Said. The colonial hangover that resulted in a distorted psyche of the colonial figure cannot be overlooked. In fact, the psychological disorders were greater than the physical subjugation of these people. Thus, they are living a life of ambivalence. The lives of the natives are trapped 'in-betweenness' and 'halfness'. They are confused between 'self' and 'other'. Mimicking tendency, alienation and homelessness are some of the major concepts that dominate the focus of the chapter. Moreover, running after borrowed culture, language and life-style in a vain hope to decolonize them-selves ultimately throws them into the ever-prevailing, ever-tormenting dejection which has already been destined for them. Finally, the researcher intends to question the validity of the term 'decolonization' dismissing the concept as vague and a mission impossible.

The chapter explores the colonial and post- colonial times in *The Mimic Man* by V.S. Naipaul and shows how colonial destruction has affected not only the political, economic or social conditions but the minds of these colonized people. It also looks into the fact, in spite of living in a 'modern', 'independent' post-colonial world, how modernity and freedom remain just meaningless words to the colonized people and they live in a false idea of de-colonizing themselves. Fanon in *The Wretched of the Earth* describes the false notion of decolonization as:

> "*Decolonization, which sets out to change the order of the world, is, obviously, a program me of complete disorder. Decolonization, as we know, is a historical process: that is to say that it cannot be understood, it cannot become intelligible nor clear to itself (27).*"

What Naipaul wants to focus in this novel is the 'barrenness'; barrenness of the colonized land and colonized people. Colonization has not only changed the physical and political conditions of the colonized land; the affects were much deeper and intense. It wounded and distorted the 'soul' of the colonized people. He writes about how these people are left devastated and confused when suddenly they are left free in a world they do not recognize. The 'modern' world was never modern to them; modernity remained just a matter of words. Colonization has uprooted people from their own roots in such a way that these people failed to relate themselves to anything afterwards, even after the colonizers left. They remained strangers in their own land.

This was the mindset that the colonizers inflicted upon the colonized. The colonizers not only captured their lands and properties, they enslaved the non-white people. They would make the colonized people serve for their purpose, for their benefits. Their entire culture, tradition, ritual and religion everything has been replaced by that of the colonizers. The colonized were forced to cut themselves off from everything that fabricated their existence and adapt to the life style of the colonizers. They were made to believe that the colonized people did not have any culture; they were not born with one. As if they just sprouted out of no-where and there were the colonizers acting to be their saviors. Therefore, the colonizers had left the colonized people no choice but to embrace whatever was being offered. The proverb 'I think, therefore I exist' did not apply to the colonized people because their thinking capacity was destroyed and overtaken by the colonizers; they could no longer rationalize. The colonized perceived the world through the eyes of the colonizers. The purpose was clear; the colonizers were playing with the colonized minds.

The Mimic Men by V.S. Naipaul is a story revolving around the life of its protagonist, Ralph Singh. The entire book is an autobiographical product of Ralph Singh where he collected the memoirs of his life. Ralph Singh is the perfect embodiment of *The Mimic Men*. From Singh's narration the readers get an insight into his life and his surroundings. The novel examines the Island of Isabella, a newly independent country in the Caribbean. Though independent, the Island failed to offer its people any sense of identity or national unity. During the colonial period the colonizers have shaped the lives of people with its rich English 'modern' culture; but this modernity did not belong to the people of the Island. It was not something they could relate themselves to. That is why when the colonizers, the people of the Island found themselves into a world they do not recognize. They suffered from dislocation, placelessness, fragmentation and a loss of identity. To read the novel from a political or materialistic point of view is not enough, the psychological damage that is created is very evident in the book which cannot be overlooked.

Ralph Singh is the ultimate mimic man of Naipaul to whom London was a 'promised land' where he could find order and 'snow' was his element. His attraction towards whiteness is revealed in the very first page of the novel when Singh expresses his opinions about the white man Mr. Shylock "suits made of cloth so fine I felt I could eat it. I had nothing but admiration. Mr. Shylock looked distinguished, like a lawyer or businessman. He had the habit of stroking the lobe of his ear and inclining his head to listen. I thought the gesture was attractive; I copied it. (*The Mimic Man* 7). Bhabha also states, though mimicry to the colonized is the "most elusive and effective strategies of colonial power and knowledge" (122), it leaves people more confused than ever "the discourse of mimicry is constructed around an ambivalence" (122). Bhabha also says that "mimicry repeats rather than represents" thus growth of an individual is not possible if one always haunts what he lacks which explains why at the end of the novel, Ralph Singh mimicry and an attraction towards the white, the English, the foreign disappoints him. Mimicry also becomes a hopeless attempt due to reasons elaborated later in this chapter which explains the sufferings of the colonized people.

Singh travels to London in order to find order as he found Isabella a place associated with chaos. Order and peace were words Singh associated with the English, the whites. Singh feels that his colonial education was one major factor which influenced him to take up a life of dislocation and alienation. As a victim of the colonial education and its curriculum Singh has always been encouraged to imitate the empire and become the 'mimic man'. Singh's colonial education has taught him to that the 'mother' country, England, is a symbol of order and that the English culture is superior than his own culture, if he had any. Singh recognized colonial mimicry but he could not help being a mimic man. At the same time Singh also realized that being a mimic man would not come to much help because he cannot be an Englishman in spite of his colonial education; one has to be born in England to be proper English. "My first memory of school is of taking an apple to the teacher. This puzzles me. We had no apple on Isabella. It must have been an orange; yet my memory insists on the apple. The editing is clearly at fault, but the edited version is all I have" (90). Thus, colonial education has made Singh a homeless man with no self- image and a confused mind.

It was in London during his period of education that he met Sandra, who was to be his wife later. Singh's sense of abandonment and domination give birth to Fanon's 'abandonment-'neurotic' when he met her. Ralph Singh's personal relationship with his wife almost resembles Naipaul's relationship with Pat who also met her at the Oxford University. Singh was attracted by Sandra's 'whiteness' and her superior attitudes which distinguished her from the other women:

> "*I had such confidence in her rapaciousness, such confidence in her as someone who could come to no harm-a superstitious reliance on her, which was part of the strength I drew from her-that in the moment it seemed to me that to attach myself to her was to acquire that protection which she offered, to share some of her quality of being marked, a quality which ones was mine but which I had lost (The Mimic Man 56).*"

Singh being the 'man of color', an attraction towards English white women who resembled power and position to him was very much expected. Singh was always reluctant to be tied into any relationship. He wanted to be in control of his relationship with the white women; it gave him a sense of power. Singh, being a non-English and a non-white, rejection has been the only attitude he received from the colonizers therefore Singh took certain pleasure in rejecting the white woman who came across his life- "I said to a French woman, 'Do you dance?' She at once rose. It was then that out of nowhere the impulse of cruelty came to me. I said, 'I don't.' and I left" (20). Singh had always been deprived of family life and family bonding because of the broken disturbed relationship he had seen between his parents. He lived a divided life, often staying with just one of his parents and away from his siblings. He had never experienced joyous family moments.

Singh's marriage with Sandra was not because he loved her, but because he "tend to marry in Europe not so much out of love as for the satisfaction of being the master of a European woman; and a certain tang of proud revenge enters into this" (Fanon 69). It is clear that Singh felt his position elevated and secured in the presence of Sandra.

His broken marriage had left him more confused and with a sense of utter failure. Ralph Singh never found the order he was searching for in London, rather he found himself into greater disorder. On returning to his Island, Singh decided to become a politician in order to fulfill his psychological need for order and an identity. "Only with The Mimic Men does the recognition of a national history in the landscape become necessary condition for establishing a stable identity" (Cooke 32). He also took up politics because he wanted to get a real view of himself, to get rid him of the "panic of ceasing to feel myself as a whole person" (33). His reasons behind joining politics were not to help his fellow Islanders but to satisfy his own ego and to feel himself in a position of power. As a politician Singh does not concentrate on helping to reduce poverty or the sufferings of the people but he was obsessed with 'naming' everything. That showed his thirst for power and ownership "So I went on naming; and later, I required everything-every government building, every road, every agricultural scheme-to be labeled. It reinforced that sense of ownership which overcame me..." (*The Mimic Man* 215). Thus, Singh was doing the same thing that once the colonizers did to the Island; he was behaving like the colonizers. Singh referred to his political activity as 'drama'. 'Drama' because all his actions as a politician only a series of experiments that he applied on the Island and the people, to satisfy his ego. It was not a real-life experience for him and he was aware that his role as a 'colonial' politician was meaningless; it was more of sarcasm. Singh writes:

> "*Politicians are people who truly make something out of nothing. They have few concrete gifts to offer. They are not engineers or artists or makers. They are manipulators; they offer themselves as manipulators. Having no gifts to offer, they seldom know what they seek. They might say they seek power. But their definition of power is vague and unreliable (43).*"

Singh's sense of drama failed and he understands that without the help and guidance of the English, the 'masters', they could not do anything. They lived in an illusion of power, but they could never escape from being the 'colonial' subject as with Mimic Men. They were mere puppets in the hands of the colonizers.

> "*My career of the colonial politician is short and ends brutally. We lack order, above all we lack power, and we do not understand that we lack power. We mistake words and the acclamation of words for power; as soon as our bluff is called, we are lost (The Mimic Man 10-11).*"

When Singh returned to the Island, he only saw hatred on the face of his people for him, "I knew that return to my island and to my political life is impossible" (10). He knew his game was over, he was seen as their betrayer and he could no longer wear a façade. It was time to Singh to escape again, "it was necessary to rise and prepare for another departure" (284).

Thus, throughout the entire novel Singh spent all his life traveling from places to places trying to find an order, a final settlement in his life. Singh realized, being the 'mimic man' would not help him find his own identity. Rather by changing his name from Ranjit Kirpal Singh to an English name, Ralph Singh, he went further away from the identity he searched for. Mimicry took away his own native identity as well as did not help him in becoming the 'white' man, "Almost the same but not white" (Bhabha 128). As the novel approaches an end and thus Singh's narrative a few things are very clear. A heterogeneous society of the Caribbean would not offer Singh any emotional or real sense of security. Moreover, through mimicry he cannot achieve a status equal to the English; he would always remain the mimic man. His marriage failed because it was loveless, he devalued the true essence of a marriage and used it as a ladder for his own benefits. Singh remembers his marriage as 'profoundly fraudulent' (*The Mimic Man* 301). To a colonial politician, politics held no meaning; they lived in an illusion of power which brought no real sense of identity or control.

To overcome all these and to find some control over his life, Singh took up writing. Through writing Singh wanted to give a picture to his chaotic mind. Writing was a means of release to him, to put his distorted life on pen and chapter so that he could look at it from a better perspective. Writing was his desperate effort to bring order and meaning to his fragmented past and put the puzzles together. Some of his 'hopeful' moments for example his departure from Isabella, his travel to London, his marriage, the beginning of his political career, all these incidents in his life where he was hopeful of a better life, an ordered future, Singh referred to these moments as 'that period in parenthesis'. As life that part of his life is long lost, as if the 'hope' was never there. That part of his life he could not relate to himself anymore. However, Singh is unable to follow a chronological order in his writing. He moves constantly backwards and forwards, from his life in Isabella to his life in London, his student life and his marriage, his childhood to adulthood and his political career. One moment Singh talks about his present and the next moment he is lost in his past. This lack of synchronization also represents Singh's internal chaos, his spiritual and psychological disturbances. He kept on jumping from one incident to another having no cohesion between events. Degrading the Island, Singh was unable to find order in London and his blind imitation of the white people failed him. He traveled from places to places in order to find a place where he could settle down but he was always aware of the 'imminent homelessness' (249).

Thus, mimicry leads Singh ultimately nowhere. The desire to overcome the difference between the natives and the foreign, one's authorization over one-self which comes from self-control is in question. Bhabha says:

> "*Mimicry does not merely destroy narcissistic authority through the repetitious slippage of difference and desire. It is the process of the fixation of the colonial as a form of cross-classificatory, discriminatory knowledge within an interdictory discourse and therefore necessarily raises the question of the authorization of colonial representations (129).*"

At the end we see Singh lacked self- control. Though he understood that mimicry would not serve his purpose, his lack of self-confidence made him the mimic man. Nevertheless, Singh had found a new insight in his life; he realized that acceptance also came with power. Accepting the fact that mimicry would not help him gave him new directions in life. He said "I have cleared the desks, as it were, and prepared myself for fresh actions. It will be the action of a free man" (*The Mimic Man* 125). Thus, the novel ends on a positive note where "far from being hopeless about the predicament of the modern West Indian and of modern man, Ralph Singh, by his example, shows how modern man can be transcend and be extended by his plastic world" (Boxill 19).

In the final analysis it is affirmed that decolonization was impossible for the colonized people because their minds and souls were colonized; there was no transformation of the soul. The colonized, understanding their own imprisonment were helpless to liberate them because they could not think anything beyond imperialism. The question which kept me wandering and with which I end my chapter is, where does the term *'post-colonialism'* place it-self? Is there such a term as 'post-colonialism'? Even if there is, where is the 'post' in it? We all still live as colonial beings in a very Western dominated world. Independence and freedom are just words which hold no meaning to the colonized subject. Perhaps the term 'post-colonialism' is also a strategy created by the colonizers which further enhance their field of illusion under which they dominate the colonized.

Works Cited

Ashcroft, Bill, Griffiths, Gareth, and Tiffin, Helen. *Post- Colonial Studies: The Key Concepts.* 2nd Ed. New York: MLA, 2007. Print.

Bhabha, Homi K. *The Location of Culture.* Routledge: New York, 1994. Print.

Boxill. Anthony. *The Little Bastard World of V.S. Naipaul's The Mimic Men and A Flag on the Island.* (1976): 12-19. *Pdf.* Web. 04 Sep. 2012.

Cooke, John. "A Vision Of The Land": V.S. Naipaul's Later Novels." *Caribbean Quarterly* 25.4 (1979): 31-47. *JSTOR.Web.* 6 March. 2013.

Fanon, Frantz. *Black Skin White Masks* . (1967): 17-82. *Pdf.* Web. 04 Sep. 2012.

Fanon, Frantz. *The Wretched of the Earth.* Penguin: London, 1967. Print.

Naipaul, V.S. *The Mimic Men.* Andre Deutsch Limited: London, 1967. Print.

Said, Edward. "Two *Visions in Heart of Darkness" Culture and Imperialism.*"(1993): 22-31. *Pdf.* Web. 04 Sep. 2012.

CHAPTER EIGHT

A Study of the Conception of Bhabhasque's Hybridity in the works of Marlon James (Suman Devi & Dr. Kumar Gaurav, LPU)

This paper will explore the works of Marlon James from the perspective of Hybridity, a postcolonial theme. In this chapter, which addresses the academic, the researchers attempt to understand Marlon James' works under the illumination of Bhabha's hybridity. Homi K. Bhabha developed his idea of Hybridity in his significant text, *The Location of Culture* (1994), where it is introduced as a Paradigm of colonial anxiety. The term is utilized in discourse about race, identity and multiculturalism. The significant proposition is the Hybridity of colonial identity. Marlon James was granted the Booker Prize for dealing with multiculturalism and the subject of Hybridity in his books. He additionally causes her characters to seem both diverse and vital to her perusers. As a component of the characters' insight, they are stood up to clashes between acclimatizing and protecting their culture. The novels of Marlon James illustrate the lives of a wide range of backgrounds, and the novels set both the objects of irony and satire, implying the need for a more nuanced reading and perception of such characters and settings. The novels' characters overflow with 'hybridity'; mixed backgrounds, various religions, and a subsequent generation of blended cultures. Though the characters inhabit such vastly different spheres, they are united and able to relate to one another through their common humanity. Marlon James's writing suggests that the reality of the past and history must be recognized to move forward.

This chapter traverses the problem of identity and Hybridity in postcolonial literature since the quest for identity and Hybridity is a significant theme in postcolonial studies and literature. The primary purpose is to examine the effects of the colonizer's dominance upon natives and how they reflect upon colonization. Hybridity has recently become one of the most steady and muddled concepts unswervingly connected with character arrangement under colonial antagonism and inequity. Homi Bhabha, as a prominent figure in contemporary cultural discourse, his hypothesis of cultural difference gives the theoretical jargon of Hybridity and the Third Space. One of the pioneers to present the idea developed from cultural and literary theory establishing his commitments on the connection between the colonizer who enticed to interpret the colonized native characters making a cultural clash. He works on the idea of 'hybridity' and features by contention the 'Third Space' presence wherein the two referenced blended societies, morals, and values meet and coincide in a solitary person after a long time of expansionism. Homi Bhabha alludes to this combination as Hybridity. Bhabha's concept of Hybridity is established on Bakhtin's idea of hybridization.

Moreover, for Bakhtin, Hybridity is defined as the double-voicedness of languages. According to his literary theory, a language can signify another while holding "the capacity to sound simultaneous both outside and within it"

(358). "Decolonization never takes place unnoticed, for it influences individuals and modifies them fundamentally" (Fanon *The Wretched* 36). Grobman explains:

> "*Hybridity does not subsume or privilege on competing forms. It enables readers to escape limiting binaries by considering the countless relationships among the text's many variables, both within and with other texts. The hybrid text is a volatile mixture of parts that work against, within, and among one another, and it is fraught with tensions and conflicts. However, these qualities offer transformative possibilities for reading, interpretation appreciation, politics and pedagogy (xiv).*"

Hybridity is anticipatorily resourceful, allowing the "creation of new transcultural forms within the contact zones produced by colonization" (Ashcroft et al. 20). In his essay, *The Location of Culture,* Bhabha states that there is a space "in-between the designations of identity " and that "this interstitial passage between fixed identifications opens up the possibility of cultural Hybridity that entertains difference without an assumed or imposed hierarchy " (4). In other words, cultural Hybridity is twisted at one condition, which is the confrontation with the colonial, i.e., at the moment, the 'Self' and 'Other' are in each other's pocket or attached.

Homi K. Bhabha is a significant thinker in the Post-Colonial Criticism and key concepts Such as hybridity, mimicry, otherness, difference and ambivalence. As per Bhabha's post, colonial theory means these terms describe how colonized people have been regulated. The power of the Colonizer. It is beyond doubt that he is the leader of postcolonial studies. His works affect a wide range of themes: Nationalism, Ethnicity, Post-Colonial Literature, Culture and philosophy of the third world countries, identity crisis etc., but the keyword to distinguish his research activity is still "Post Colonialism". Homi K. Bhabha developed his concept of Hybridity in his key text, *The Location of Culture* (1994), where it is presented as a Paradigm of colonial anxiety. He used this concept to describe culture and identity construction within conditions of imbalance and antagonism.

Bhabha expresses his relationship between culture and Hybridity, which is one of the central issues of this study. As per Bhabha, Hybridity is the process the colonial overseeing authority embraces to decipher the identity of the colonized (the others). Within a solitary general framework, but then fails to create something familiar but new. It is an evocative term for the formation of identity. This idea has been taken from Edward Said's Work *Orientalism*, which describes the emergence of new cultural forms of multiculturalism. Homi Bhabha generated the concept of Hybridity in terms of culture, which refers to the mixedness of culture. Every culture is an original mixedness within every form of identity. According to Bhabha, It is a combination of two or more identities within one person without an assumed or imposed hierarchy. It is a mixture of the colonized experience and the colonized influence. The term hybridity originated from biology and was employed in linguistics and racial theory in the 19th century. The terms are used in discourses about race identity and multiculturalism. The significant proposition is the Hybridity of colonial identity. It is a process of cultural exchange. Briefly, Hybridity is the concept in the colonized country that mainly talks about how cultural blends happen in the colonized country. It is also designated as a sign of colonial supremacy, which controls the colonized people's behaviour and ethos and shows the colonizer's superior ethos.

Postcolonial theory and studies' most disputable and notable issue is the quest for identity or identity crisis. Postcolonial theorists have considered the obstacle of identity as one of the significant impacts of colonialism on regional culture. It is the most pressing problem in postcolonial time and literature and the most imperative for its crisis in postcolonial communities that tackled newly freed nations in their quest for identity. Identity is marked as "the certainty of being who or what a man or thing is" as per oxford English definition of identity. Frantz Fanon and Edward Said perceive identity crisis as influenced by the colonial impact on colonized people, making them feel minor and inferior. As per Frantz Fanon, an identity crisis is a historical association between the colonized and colonizers. On the contrary, Edward Said associated the identity crisis with political discourse. His thoughts are established on the Foucaultian view of power and knowledge; Said interprets the relationship between the colonized countries and the colonial power and individuals.

The postcolonial writers uncovered the dilemma of identity and the problems associated with identity. Marlon James is one of the remarkable postcolonial novelists. His novels exhibit the struggle to find an identity as a slaved person or a postcolonial inhabitant of Jamaica. He dispenses the anguish of Postcolonial society struggling for its own identity. His first novel *John Crow's Devil* explores postcolonial Jamaica through a religiously battle between good and evil. In this novel, James deploys a small community show to present the more considerable misery of a postcolonial society struggling with its own identity, but he immersed this with religious ardour. The ghost of colonialism is precise, but the instability and strive for identity are clear to the reader. His next novel, *The Book of Night Women,* also deals with the quest for identity as an enslaved of Jamaica.

John Crow's Devil, the first novel, is set in 1957, five years before the autonomy of Jamaica, in the fictional village of Gibeah, Jamaica. In this book, there is a battle between two men for the position of the town's singular religious leader. Hector Bligh, a preacher in the small town of Gibeah in Jamaica, battled with liquor addiction and acquired the nickname "The Rum preacher". One day Apostle York, a brimstone preacher, unexpectedly appears and forcefully removes Bligh from the pulpit and harshly beats him. Bligh come back to the congregation to find that his mass no longer needs him, and York is willing to retreat violence to repel him. His next novel, *The Book of Night Women,* Lilith, was born into slavery.

Marlon James follows the existence of Jamaican enslaved ladies during the British colonization of the Caribbean Island. James tries to describe from the women's perspective in general and enslave women particularly. He does not elude associating women with violence. They view as observers, culprits, and casualties of violence. In the novel In T*he book of night women*, brutality is constrained by gender. James emphasized the extreme violence of British Colonial rule and slavery. In this novel, he traversed one of the darkest and most painful chapters of the Caribbean and modern history. The novel focuses on the fate of Lilith (daughter of a slave woman) and a tyrannical white overseer Jack Wilkins. This novel inspects the white colonial rule and the complex history of slavery in Jamaica during the eighteenth century. The novel *The Book of Night Women* is intertextual to work with *The Wretched of the Earth* by Frantz Fanon to eradicate violence by using more violence.

John Crow's Devil, his first novel, is set in 1957, in the fictional town of Gibeah, Jamaica, five years before the autonomy of Jamaica. There is a battle between two people for the town's singular religious pioneer in this novel. Hector Bligh, a preacher in the little town of Gibeah in Jamaica, fought with alcohol compulsion and gained the nickname "The Rum preacher". One day a brimstone preacher, Apostle York, startlingly shows up and fiercely eliminates Bligh from the platform and severely beats him. The assembly attracted York's leads as he filled the otherworldly vacuum left by Bligh's unfilled and courteous service. Bligh returns to the gathering to find that his array never again needs him, and York will withdraw brutality to repulse him. His resulting novel, The Book of Night Women, accompanies Lilith, naturally introduced to subjugation. Marlon James follows the presence of Jamaican slave women during the British colonization of the Caribbean Island. James endeavours to explicitly depict, according to ladies' point of view, slave ladies. He does not try to connect ladies with brutality. They view as guilty parties, onlookers and losses from viciousness. In the book of night ladies, ruthlessness is compelled by orientation. James featured the outrageous cruelty of bondage and British Colonial rule. In this book, he investigated one of the haziest and most excruciating sections of the Caribbean and present-day history. The story centers around the destiny of Lilith (girl of a slave lady) and an overbearing white manager Jack Wilkins. This novel investigates the local white rule and the perplexing history of subjection in Jamaica during the eighteenth 100 years. *The Book of Night Women* remains intertextual to Frantz Fanon's work *The Wretched of the Earth,* to destroy brutality by utilizing more viciousness.

A postcolonial writer such as Marlon James sought to depict these notions, identity and Hybridity, by carefully representing the elements that make up these concepts of identity, such as language, characters, religion, style, setting, and home culture, etc. Interestingly, what creates a debate over the representation of postcolonial societies is that many postcolonial writers write about the experience of their people in foreign languages, mainly that of their colonizers. Next to identity lies Hybridity, a critical element explored by Marlon James. He depicts cultural Hybridity through their characters as different in how they live and correspond. In most postcolonial prose, there is the notion of mixing cultures; however, people resist ultimately adopting the new regimes at the expense of their original identity. For example, they portray their characters as hybrids by dressing, communicating, behaving, etc. But still, other characters seem to act on the opposite side, rebelling against the changes. Marlon James, through their literature, declares in one way or another that Hybridity is alive within their society and that people during and after colonization are becoming inevitably multicultural people and their endeavours to regain the purity of their identity are quite impossible.

Conclusion

According to what has been mentioned and discussed above, Hybridity changed the structure of society. It was successful in releasing the multicultural characteristics that were fought for vigorously. It neutralized the need to control others, as shown during colonial times and offered every person an opportunity to lead or manage. Nonetheless, as it created opportunities on one side, on the other side, confusion was created, which enhanced the lack of identity. The novelist Marlon James uses many elements that help create a successful novel that depicts the life of the immigrants and the refugees. The construction of the individual's identity and the state of Diaspora, and the dilemma of self-determination are the main focuses of Smith in her novel. He vividly shows the suffering of the people of different origins, represented by the misrecognition and racism that the white society adopted in its treatment of them when calling them "different". The novelist succeeded in drawing a complete picture of the identity structure in a community distinguished by its various cultures, races, and religions. Creating an identity in such a society is not an easy task. It has many aspects that cause suffering for the individuals that live in such a society. Writing the novel aims to illustrate this suffering, which is fully achieved.

Works Cited

Bakhtin, M. M., and Michael Holquist. *The Dialogic Imagination: Four Essays.* University of Texas Press, 2000.

Bhabha, Homi K. *The Location of Culture.* Routledge, 1994.

Bill, Ashcroft et al. *Key Concepts in Postcolonial Studies.* London: Routledge, 1998.

Fanon, Frantz. *The Wretched of the Earth.* Translated by Constance Farrington. New York Grove P, 1968

Grobman, Laurie. *Multicultural hybridity: Transforming American Literary Scholarship and Pedagogy* Urbana, IL: NCTE, 2007.

James, Marlon. *A Brief History of Seven Killings.*Great Britain: Oneworld Publications, 2015.

---. *The Book of Night Women.* Great Britain: Oneworld Publications, 2014.

---. *Black Leopard, Red Wolf: Dark Star Trilogy Book 1.* Riverhead Books Publications, 2019.

---. *John Crow's Devil.* London: Oneworld Publications, 2005.

CHAPTER NINE

Cultural Trauma and Identity Crisis: A Psychoanalytic Study of Bapsi Sidhwa's Select Novels (Dr. Poonam Sareen, TPDM College, Punjab University)

'Why for one lost home mourn, when grief

Can find so many a lodging place?'

(From a *ghazal* in *Bal-i-Jibril* by Mohammad Iqbal, translated By V.G. Kiernan)

Bapsi Sidhwa a prominent diasporic novelist, hailing from the minority community of Parsis in Pakistan, but now settled in America has remarkably accomplished the role of a writer as the preserver of different cultures, traditions and modernism. She has been highly regarded as a feminist postcolonial writer who effectively discusses the issues of cultural differences in her works. Immigration and cultural hybridity are the recurring themes in her novels. Through her narrative writings, she has portrayed the psyche (the yearnings, anxieties, confusion and aspirations) of the immigrants. In her maiden novel, *The Crow Eaters* (TCE 2001) published in 1978 Sidhwa represented the migratory nature of her community, their adaptability, eccentricity, ethnic customs, rituals and religious beliefs through her character Faredoon Jungle Walla. In her later novels, she has illustrated intercultural undulations and their psychological impacts on the emigrants. Her own experience of being in different countries stands out as it depicts the process of assimilation and alienation of her characters from the transnational perspective. Positioning her characters in a variety of social and cultural milieus, Sidhwa has represented their multiple identities. Both of her novels *The Pakistani Bride and An American Brat* deal with themes of cross-cultural conflicts and fully justifies diasporic sensibilities. According to Clifford (1994), Diaspora is associated "...with the idea of particular sentiments towards the homeland, whilst being formed by those of the place of settlement. This place is one where one is constructed in and through difference, and yet is one that produces differential forms of cultural accommodation or syncretism: in some versions, hybridity." Diasporic community aim at being similar as well as different from the host cultures. It results in hybridization and syncreticity. Feroza in *An American Brat* attempts to maintain her cultural identity and at the same time tries to get assimilated into American society by adopting its social practices and codes of behavior.

The concept of trauma has different perspectives in various academic fields like literature, sociology, psychology, and cultural studies. The early stage of trauma concepts and formulated ideas on trauma are seen from a psychological point of view that focuses on an individual than a collective form. Jeffery C. Alexander describes cultural trauma as "Cultural trauma occurs when members of a collectivity feel they have been subjected to a horrendous event that leaves indelible marks upon their group consciousness, marking their memories forever and changing their future identity in fundamental and irrevocable ways (1) The dislocation and displacement from native country to another country leads to trauma. Generally, due to migration an individual or a community faces an identity crisis and suffers in terms of their distorted culture.

An examination of Bapsi Sidhwa's works *The Pakistani Bride and An American Brat* explore the psyche of the expatriate in a contrasting way. In *The Pakistani Bride,* Carol who belongs to Britain comes to Pakistan with her husband and thus experiences the cruel and repressive culture of Pakistan whereas in *An American Brat* there is Firoza Ginwalla who is born into a society with restrictive social and political codes, moves to America and observes the cultural shift due to the territorial shift which resulted in her overlapping identity. Thus, both the novels reveal the hybridization and intricacy of different communities.

Sidhwa is a keen observer who delicately points out contrasting codes of conduct of these nations by putting her characters in them. *The Pakistani Bride* reflects the repression of women in the conventional cultural society of Pakistan. The tension created due to these cross-cultural values lead us to the ill-fated story of Zaitoon and Carol, the two female protagonists of the novel. Zaitoon, an orphan girl, is brought up by Qasim as her own daughter. Her story haunts us with the harsh value system of the tribal community of northwest regions of Pakistan which reveals how the honour of a man is judged by how well he can oppress his women. The rebellious reaction of Zaitoon towards her tortured married life shows her contrasting attitude as compared to the adaptive one of Feroza in *An American Brat.* Carol on the other hand represents a typically middle-class American woman. She gets married to Farukh, a Pakistani engineer, who brings her to Pakistan along with him. Her confrontations with a society of different value systems subvert her identity and her psychology as a woman in a strange land.

An American Brat focuses on how various modalities, such as gender, race, class, religion and language destabilize the identity of a person. The protagonist Feroza is introduced to the readers from contrasting social and cultural tendencies across time and space. In the opening chapters of the novels, Feroza is a very diffident orthodox girl which worries her mother Zareen as this behavior is implausible in their Parsis community. Shocked by this attitude she complains about this to her husband by saying:

> "*I went to bring Feroza from school today. I was chatting with Mother Superior on the veranda – she was out enjoying the Sun – and I had removed my cardigan. Feroza pretended she didn't know me. In the car she said- "Mummy please don't come to school dressed like that." She objected to my sleeveless sari blouse! This narrow-minded attitude touted by General Zia is infecting her, too. I told her: Look, we're Parsi, everybody knows we dress differently.(10)*"

This incident reveals the conservative and timid behavior of Feroza which according to her mother is due to the influence of Islamic fundamentalism. With this background in our mind, Sidhwa presents the protagonist in a claustrophobic narrow-minded social structure of Pakistan. To broaden her outlook Zareen sends her to America to her uncle Manek who can assist her in getting exposure to a different culture. This is the turn from where Feroza's perceptions are shattered and her ideas are re-conceptualized.

Self-dependence and hard work which are the key factors of survival in a country like America have been beautifully exposed when Manek teaches Feroza about this by saying:

> "*The first lesson you learn in America is „you don't get something for nothing, " Manek said. "If you want to get into the right college you have to work for it. Nothing is given to you on a plate. You don't know that because nobody works in Pakistan. Not your father, your grandfathers or uncles." (124)*"

In contrast with the Pakistani social milieu, working conditions in America is also illustrated when it is told that Husband and wife both works. Every minute is organized. A wife will say, "Dear, put the clothes in the washing machine and come back in ten minutes to take our son to the baseball practice. I'll be back from the grocery store in thirty minutes to put the clothes in the dryer and take our daughter to ballet lessons. (124)

Feroza's notions about America are further widened when she is exposed to museums, libraries and shopping malls where she wonders at the quick services and the quantities of fries, ketchup, and the ice in the coke. The greatness of Sidhwa as an artist lies in the fact, she sometimes conceptualizes diaspora as a form of cultural disparagement too. Novy Kapadia observes, "Creditably during this initial phase of the novel, Sidhwa does not emerge as an apologist for the first world or the USA. She chronicles the glamour and efficiency of the USA but also delineates the seedy and violent aspects of life in a post-industrial, consumerist and technology-dominated society." (189)

An example of it is when Feroza is struck in a dark stairway which is an ugly experience for her to be accepted. "Feroza felt disoriented, confused for a moment about where she was. The air was rank with the odor of stale cigarette smoke and food. She got a whiff of urine and of decaying refuse." (88)

This experience weathered the pain of culture shock which hinders her efforts to get accustomed to the host country. Her reaction to this fearful incident symbolizes the trauma of displacement in an alien country. Her encounter with the harsh realities of the First World shatters her preconceptions about America.

The smell of New York repels her and she struggled to adjust to the poverty and stench of the filth of the First World This was alien filth, a compost reeking of vomit and alcoholic belches, of neglected old age and sickness, of drugged exhalations and the Malodorous ferment of other substances she could not decipher. The smells disturbed her psyche; it seemed to her they personified the callous heart of the rich country that allowed such savage neglect to occur. (81)

Disseminating the social constructs among the migrants, Sidhwa portrays the values of America in a wider sense. Feroza adopts the language of her roommate Jo and learns some new words which are objectionable in her native country. Feroza saying "shit" and "ass hole" with an abandon that epitomized for her the heady reality of her being abroad, away from home, and even if she knew it was an illusion, a sense of control over her actions." (159)

Similarly, the sexual liberty in America presented by Bapsi Sidhwa in *An American Brat* shows her genius for closely viewing the socio-cultural values of a country. She delves into the psyche of the immigrant to understand her emotions. The confusion and remorse produced as a result of this fluidity in sexual behavior is portrayed beautifully in the novel. As Feroza finds herself engaged in dating David, with whom she falls in love and wants to marry, she was driven by the guilt of doing so as this involvement is prohibited in her culture. "Once, when she was sneaking back into her room at three o'clock in the morning, with her shoes in her hand, she wondered if she was the same girl, who had lived in Lahore and gone to the Convent of the Sacred Heart." (264)

Similarly, the theme of intercultural marriage is also discussed in the novel. Feroza's decision to marry David, a Jewish boy, is condemned by her Parsi society. Zareen rushes to America to dissuade her daughter from marrying a person of another religion. After meeting David, Zareen realizes that he is a sensible attractive suitable boy for her daughter. She regrets her own traditions and customs which make them narrow-minded. Hence, the rigidity of the rituals of a particular community is condemned in the novel.

The Pakistani Bride also reveals the same picture of malign and envious behavior of a particular tribal community of Pakistan in contrast to the sophisticated and gentile attitude of the other. Bapsi Sidhwa's own multicultural background allows her to mix different cultures in her novels. She creates transnational spaces by combining both her Pakistani and American identities. *The Pakistani Bride* highlights the cultural mechanism at work in the heart of Pakistani society. Here again, the contrasting cultural values of Pakistan and America are compared. While Zaitoon suffers from the possessiveness of her husband, Carols get involved in extramarital affairs with her husband's friend, Major Mustaf. The cruel treatment, the beatings and mistrust in Zaitoon's married life are due to the brutal and orthodox value system of her community. On the other hand, Carol enjoys sex with Major Mustaf due to her inclination of enjoying sexual liberty in her native country. But soon Carol realizes the wrong notion of Major who only values her as a sexual object. This helps her in the assimilation of her husband's social values. She begins to understand Zaitoon's conditions well and starts feeling affection for her husband and their loveless life. Later she plans to conceive to add meaning to her married life. To make her novel explicable to western readers Sidhwa weaves together Carol's disappointment with alien culture with Zaitoon's tragedies. Finally, when Carol finds it impossible to survive in this culture, she decides to go back to America.

Carol gets convinced that she cannot take it anymore. She suddenly remembers Zaitoon. Zaitoon had exercised her "Khudi" and now it is time for her to do the same— "I think I'm finally beginning to realize something ... Your civilization ... has ways that really hurt me ... I'm going home." With this pronouncement, Carol goes back to America.(229)

Thus, Sidhwa's *The Pakistani Bride* focuses on the phenomenon of migration involving dislocation and relocation. It reveals the truth about the common values prevailing in a community that is out of touch with the world. Hence it portrays Sidhwa's observing concern for the moral and psychological truth related to the immigrant's discontentment with the culture they are put into.

From the above discussion, it can be concluded that Bapsi Sidhwa's *The Pakistani Bride and An American Brat* have been successfully able to bring out the predicaments of the characters who get entrapped between two cultures one inherited and the other encountered. Both Feroza, a young, strong-willed and spirited Pakistani Parsi girl who is able to get assimilated into the host society and Carol, a sophisticated, independent middle-class American who fails to acclimatize to a displaced culture, portrays their expatriate experience and their struggles to outgrow inherited values. Hence description on the cover page of *An American Brat* truly justifies diasporic writer Bapsi Sidhwa as one who "divides her time between the United States where she teaches and Lahore where she lives". And her works stand out as they highlight the intercultural undulations and explain emigrant psychology. Sidhwa's books are crowded with detail and humor. She herself acclaims "I would describe myself as Punjabi-Pakistani-Parsi woman.... I actually have a whole medley of identities." (183)

Works Cited

Alexander, Jeffrey C. "Toward a Theory of Cultural Trauma". Alexander et al. Cultural Trauma and Collective Identity. Berkeley: University of California Press, 2004.

Clifford, James. "Diasporas", *Cultural Anthropology*, vol. 9, No. 3.1994.

Sidhwa, Bapsi, *An American Brat,* New Delhi: Penguin Books India Pvt. Ltd., 1994.

Kapadia, Novy, "Expatriate Experience and Theme of Marriage" in *An American Brat, The Novels of Bapsi Sidhwa,* Ed. R. K. Dhawanand Novy Kapadia, New Delhi: Prestige Books, 1996.

Sidhwa, Bapsi. *The Pakistani Bride.* Minneapolis, Minnesota: Milkweed Editions, 1983.

Sidhwa, Bapsi quoted by Patrick M.O'Neil. in *Great World Writers: Twentieth Century,* New York: Marshal Cavendish, 2004.

CHAPTER TEN

Interdisciplinary Cultural Episteme: A Critical Study of Tale of Two Cities, Lord of The Flies and Train to Pakistan (Pooja Kumari, PhD, LPU)

There is a strong bond between literature and other disciplines in one way or the other. The paper reflects the application of interdisciplinary ideas to literary text which gives a deep meaning and novelty to the piece of creation. It helps make a piece of art to become more valuable, creative, relevant and impressive. Approach to other disciplines like sociology, economics, political theories, linguistics, psychology, history and many more, give shape to literary text. This topic has gained a wide attention of scholars been a lot of discussion. It permits text to cross the traditional boundaries of writing. Although this term remained in trend for a long time, nowadays it is gaining popularity at a wide range. This emerging field of English literature demands an awareness of other disciplines. Novel which is considered to be far from reality, takes its base from authors' background and sensibility and experiences based on social, historical, psychological, and geographical aspects. And without the knowledge of other disciplines, it's hard to understand the text, specifically humanities to cover thoughts of text for an exact understanding. Understanding of other disciplines makes it easier and more comprehensible for us to be familiar with literary text.

Reading a literary text involves considerations of its writer's views and era in which it was designed, the social, political surroundings and religious thoughts of that age. Relying on dominants themes in text, the reader and writer dives into several aspects like history, philosophy, economics, sociology, psychology, politics and sciences. Film study is also another area that cannot be ignored. In this sense interdisciplinary study is soul of English literature.

There is wide arena of works in English literature which is covered with the variety of different disciplines. Interdisciplinary approach has given these works a perfect form. The simplest example of interdisciplinary approach may be found within text which is interlinked containing history in literary text. To analyze literary text, understanding of history is fundamental. The most popular novel *A Tale of Two Cities, written* by Charles Dickens is reflection of French Revolution in history. To understand the work completely, knowledge of history is required. The novel shows a picture of the time from 1757 to 1794, and for making a proper understanding of this piece of literature, a complete and comprehensive knowledge of particular time of French Revolution and Industrial Revolution would be required. The story would be complete with comprehensive knowledge of particular history of France during that age of flux. Dickens researched the revolution extensively before writing his knowledge and shows remarkable pictures of that revolution accurately. Dickens another novel, *Hard Times* is considered comprehensive when it is colored in flavor of Industrial Era and social Flux in England.

Another example dealing with the correlation of interdisciplinary and literature is Khushwant Singh's *Train to Pakistan*. It evokes historical aspects of partition time which segregated a sub-continent into India and Pakistan. While talking about historical issues of partition, the teacher exemplifies novel *Train to Pakistan* by Khushwant Singh. This novel presents a complete picture of the that time in which India was divided into two parts on the basis of religion and culture so that unfamiliar person may get complete understanding of that the time to understand the text fully. All traditions of people like the Sikhs, the Hindu and the Muslims have been considered as the part of the text. It seems to be real as if history is being alive to tell the tales of cruelty, destruction and migration. Through the characters real human pictures and actions have been depicted. Government's decision, and its impact on masses brings a base to novel. Political science, sociology, geography and history paves the way of understanding of text and no literary text can be understood in isolation. To achieve complete aesthetic values of literary text we have to rely on multidisciplinary approach. The novel narrates story of human aspects related to political, historical and geographical factors. It presents horrible picture of partition. The story tells us about Sikh character Jugga, who is a goon and feels attracted towards Nooran, a Muslim girl. The communal tension of Hindus and Muslims and Sikhs brought destruction for all. They blame each other, stabbed each other, shot each other and tortured each other (Singh 1). Thus, the history becomes an integral part of literature to reiterates the complicated ties between culture and literary text. The glimpses of partition also talk about the psychological dilemma and trauma of human beings who migrated to unknown soil leaving their mother land.

Another work holding interdisciplinary aspect with itself is *Lord of The Flies* a beautiful creation of *William Golding*. The novel has philosophical aspects as its theme. The basic idea of the fiction is war between two opposite side instincts which lie in everyman: the desire to rule over others the, work calmly, accept ethical values follow, and value the good of others against desire to satisfy one's instant desire, act harshly to gain power to rule over others, and to win someone's will. Two main characters, who are leaders in the story, have different characteristics, motives and objectives. They adopt their own ways to maintain discipline and rule the boys. The selected and chosen leader is Ralph while Jack is self-appointed leader. In starting they work towards common purposes but gradually the difference of views creates a conflict among them. In the very beginning of the novel Ralph takes the responsibility of group's tasks to organize their life. After some time, he starts to feel his supremacy among others as he makes, they feel safe under his aegis. He is elected in a democratic manner. Ralph is a compassionate character who cares for all and all boys support the rule and order set by him. Butas sometime passes this order starts to be disordered and all chooses to live in easiest way. The boys want to get freedom and fun by hunting and playing. On other side we find Jack who is arrogant, authoritarian and savage declares himself to be a perfect leader for boys. He soon, starts different strategies to undermine Ralph's authority, and at the same moment making him more powerful. He breaks rules set by former leader and spread evil in the veil of freedom. Golding's philosophical views about values are clearly shown in this work.

Psychology is another factor which can be seen as an example of interdisciplinary correlation in literary text. This kind of literature throws a sight into the inner side of characters rather than external actions and events of characters. *Crime and Punishment* by Fyodor Dostoevsky published in 1866 is the earliest psychological novel. The story of this novel moves around psychology of characters. The novels which deal with psychology are works in which memories, thinking, flow of feelings, and motivation of protagonists fetch greater interest and attention than outer scenes and events of narratives. This type of story carries the emotional stress and flow inside heart of the characters. It is affected by internal thoughts. *Hamlet by* William Shakespeare *is* surely the superb image in dramatic form. *Pamela (1740),* written by Samuel Richardson is told from the heroine's point of view, and Laurence Sterne's first-person introspective novel *Tristram Shandy (1759-67),* are commendable novels reflecting psychology of characters. It has got enrich with the development of psychology and the inventions of Sigmund Freud. Psychology brought a lot of new theories and dimensions in literature. To understand psychological literary texts in English literature like *Mrs. Dalloway, Clarrisa, The Silent Patient, and The Girl on the Train* acquaintance with psychology is mandatory. We must know about theories of psychology. Otherwise, we will not be able to find the real meaning of text.

CONCLUSION

Thus, it can be said that literature is reflection and product of its age which has many social, political, sociological, psychological, historical and geographical aspects. So interdisciplinary hermeneutic or understanding of other disciplines are mandatory to understand nature of text. Literature cannot exist in isolation. Keeping in mind, several works of literature, it can be said that scholars of literature contextualize the text within its historical, social, political, and psychological milieu. It provides chances to explain analyze and interpret area from beyond narrow zone and perspectives to a wider critical approach which is very help to dissolve lines between various fields and streams of literature.

Works cited

Cowasjee, Saros& Vasant A. Shahane (Eds.). (1981). *Modern Indian fiction.* New Delhi: Vikas Publishing House.Dickens, Charles (1859). *A tale of two cities.* Retrieved October 20, 2013

Dickens, Charles (1905). *Hard times.* Retrieved October20,1983

Griffin, Gabriele (2005). *Research methods for English studies.* Edinburgh: Edinburgh Univ. Press.

Mehrotra, Arvind Krishna. (2008). *A concise history of Indian literature in English.* New Delhi: Orient Blackswan.

Manto, Saadat Hassan. (1997). *Mottled dawn: Fifty sketches of partition.* New Delhi: Penguin Books.

Nayyar, Pramod K. (2008). *An introduction to cultural studies.* New Delhi: Viva Books.

Singh, Khushwant. (2012). *Train to Pakistan.* New Delhi: Ravi Dayal. (Original work published 1956.

CHAPTER ELEVEN

MENTAL HEALTH OF DISABLED PERSONS DURING COVID-19 (MUDASIR AHMAD WANI, RESEARCH SCHOLAR, LPU)

Disability and mental health are two important constructs that play an important role in every person's life. These two terms go hand in hand, people who are suffering from any kind of disability face a lot of heddles and road blocks in their lives. Previous researches find out that disabled persons are suffering from various psychological problems such as depression, anxiety, and stress and during the current pandemic situation (COVID-19) these issues are increasing rapidly. So, it is very important to take care of mental health issues of disabled persons during the contemporary times.

There is a developing worldwide mental health movement all over the world today (Cohen, Patel & Minas 2014) and the worldwide church is starting to perceive mental health issues, which are the main source of disability overall — more debilitating than such circumstances as coronary illness, stroke, or diabetes as a significant service need (World Health Organization, 2016).

Mental health issues are normally the aftereffect of a mix of many variables, including family environment, biology, character, other worldliness, and testing local area settings, including destitution and viciousness. Progressively, the effects of horrendous mishaps, for example, childhood abuse, interpersonal violence, or natural disasters are being recognized as major causes of mental health problems.

A new report found that grown-ups with disabilities report encountering more mental pain than those without disabilities (Cree, Okoro, Zack & Carbone, 2020). In 2018, an expected 17.4 million (32.9%) grown-ups with inabilities experienced continuous mental misery, characterized as at least 14 detailed intellectually unhealthy days in the beyond 30 days. Incessant mental distress is related with poor health behaviors, increased use of health services, mental disorders, chronic disease, and limitations in daily life (Cree *at el.*, 2020). During the COVID-19 pandemic, isolation, disconnect, disrupted routines, and diminished health services have greatly impacted the lives and mental well-being of people with disabilities (International Day of People with Disabilities, 2020).

Actually, whether the condition is a physical issue or a physical or psychological instability, living with a handicap generally shapes your life experiences. However, tolerating, and in any event, embracing, one's inability as an aspect of one's character doesn't mean submitting to a pessimist outlook. It is feasible to accommodate your experiences with injury and disease into a sound self-awareness, empowering your inability to shape what your identity is. It starts, however, by figuring out the connection among handicap and emotional well-being.

Healthy Ways to Cope with Stress

Know what to do on the off chance that you are wiped out and are worried about COVID-19. Contact a health provider before you start any self-treatment for COVID-19. Know where and how to seek psychological wellness treatment and other help administrations and assets, including directing or treatment (face to face or through tele health administrations).

Deal with your emotional health will help you think plainly and respond to dire necessities to safeguard yourself and your loved ones. Enjoy reprieves from watching, perusing, or paying attention to reports, remembering those for virtual entertainment. Finding out about the pandemic more than once can agitate. Deal with your body. Take full breaths, stretch, or meditate external symbol. Attempt to practice good eating habits, even suppers. Work-out routinely.

Get a lot of rest. Keep away from inordinate liquor and medication use Associate with others. Converse with individuals you trust about your interests and how you are feeling. During seasons of expanded social removing, individuals can in any case keep up with social associations and care for their psychological well-being. Calls or video talks can assist you and your friends and family with feeling socially associated, less forlorn, or secluded. Associate with your local area or religious associations. While social separating measures are set up, consider interfacing on the web, through web-based entertainment, or by telephone or mail.

Disability, Mental Health and Society

There is a critical assemblage of proof that people with incapacities are at an expanded gamble for self-destruction or self-destructive ideation. Not with standing, the proof likewise shows that it is not the handicapping condition fundamentally that most frequently prompts self-destructive motivations. Rather, it's the social limitations that such countless individuals with inabilities consistently face that can prompt hazardous sorrow and badly effect on their mental health. Research shows, for instance, individuals with inabilities experience gigantic hindrances to "ordinary" social working that have barely anything to do with the injury or disease itself. This incorporates boundaries that are both underlying and philosophical, from restricted admittance to public transportation or curbside patterns for wheelchair-clients to the absence of adaptable work choices for people who could require it. People with noticeable incapacities, for example, report that they frequently experience different types of separation when out in the open and previous researches find out that social isolation and mental health are negatively correlated with each other and increased the mobility risk in the persons suffering from any kind of disability (Holt et al., 2010). This incorporates the inclination for aliens to utilize the sharp tones frequently held for babies while addressing grown-ups with incapacities, to address the individual's friend or chaperon as opposed to the individual oneself, or to allude to people with inabilities as "excellent" or "gallant."

In the working environment, the misguided judgment that recruiting an individual with an incapacity would require restrictively costly facilities, or essentially that an individual with a physical issue or disease wouldn't have the option to be just about as useful or solid as a non-handicapped representative, adds to the lopsidedly high paces of joblessness among people with inabilities. As a matter of fact, as indicated by ongoing evaluations, the November 2020 work investment rate for grown-ups with handicaps was 33%, contrasted and 75% for non-debilitated grown-ups in a similar period.

Works Cited

A. Cohen, V. Patel, & H. Minas, 'A Brief History of Global Mental Health' in A. Cohen, V. Patel, H. Minas, & M.J. Prince (Eds)., *Global Mental Health: Policies and Practices* (London: Oxford University Press, 2014). ↥

Cree RA, Okoro CA, Zack MM, Carbone E (2020). Frequent Mental Distress Among Adults by Disability Status, Disability Type, and Selected Characteristics – United States 2018. Morbidity and Mortality Weekly Report (MMWR).

Holt-Lunstad, J., Smith, T. B., & Layton, J. B. (2010). Social relationships and mortality risk: a meta-analytic review. *PLoS medicine*, *7*(7), e1000316.

International Day of People with Disabilities. Accessed November 17, 2020. https://idpwd.org/external icon

World Health Organization, 'Mental Health: Strengthening Our Response Fact Sheet' (2016),http://www.who.int/mediacentre/factsheets/fs220/en/↑

World Health Organization. (2016). Global report on diabetes: executive summary.

9 798887 834337

Printed by Libri Plureos GmbH in Hamburg,
Germany